Beyond
Positive Thinking

BEYOND POSITIVE THINKING

Mind-Power Techniques for Discovering How Extraordinary You Really Are!

Patricia L. Mischell

A SPECTRUM BOOK

Prentice-Hall, Inc., Englewood Cliffs, New Jersey 07632

Library of Congress Cataloging in Publication Data

Mischell, Patricia.
  Beyond positive thinking.

  "A Spectrum Book."
  Bibliography: p.
  Includes index.
  1. Success.   I. Title.
BJ1611.2.M52 1985   131   85-3469
ISBN 0-13-071887-4
ISBN 0-13-071879-3 (pbk.)

    1   2   3   4   5   6   7   8   9   10

ISBN 0-13-071887-4

ISBN 0-13-071879-3 {PBK.}

Editorial/production supervision by Joyce Levatino
Cover design by Hal Siegel
Manufacturing buyer: Carol Bystrom

This book is available at a special discount when ordered in
bulk quantities. Contact Prentice-Hall, Inc., General
Publishing Division, Special Sales, Englewood Cliffs, N.J. 07632.

Prentice-Hall International (UK) Limited, *London*
Prentice-Hall of Australia Pty. Limited, *Sydney*
Prentice-Hall Canada Inc., *Toronto*
Prentice-Hall Hispanoamericana, S.A., *Mexico*
Prentice-Hall of India Private Limited, *New Delhi*
Prentice-Hall of Japan, Inc., *Tokyo*
Prentice-Hall of Southeast Asia Pte. Ltd., *Singapore*
Whitehall Books Limited, *Wellington, New Zealand*
Editora Prentice-Hall do Brasil Ltda., *Rio de Janeiro*

To my daughters, Cynthia and René, and my son, Steven,
for their willingness to share their lives with me.

Contents

Preface

Before you turn the page . . .

You have not picked up this book by accident; you turn its pages by divine appointment. You will find that you personally are this book's center and purpose. *Beyond Positive Thinking* promises to meet your needs, not through any human excellence or literary uniqueness, but because in this frightening nuclear age it offers you a sane, sure, satisfying answer to the intertwining problems of the mind, soul, and spirit.

Are you frequently cynical, inconsiderate, rude, or cruel? Have you tried but found it impossible to integrate positive thinking into your life? If so, this book will teach you mind techniques to change your way of thinking and guide you to a level far beyond positive thinking. You will learn how to cancel negative statements, maintain a positive outlook, and release deep-seated hatred or fears.

If you are seeking inner peace, this book will give you an easy-to-read blueprint for lasting tranquility and harmony. If you need a healing of your body as well as your spirit, learn from my personal experience exactly how to heal yourself through the powers of your mind and your Higher Self. Once you start following the Sixteen Steps to Better Health, you will begin to feel like a new person.

Are you drifting along, uncertain, indecisive? Is your life regulated by situations you feel helpless to change? If so, this book will show you how to take charge of your life. By using the Goal and Success Planner, you will become a confident decision maker who follows through on your high expectations for your own life.

If you find the hopelessness, stress, and burdens of your life unbearable, exchange hopelessness for hope by taking charge of your ideas. Realize that as a child of the Infinite Intelligence you are meant to claim your inheritance—joy, love, happiness, and prosperity. You are not meant to suffer poverty or deprivation. As you read, you will frequently identify with many of the situations and ideas in this book. You will find yourself thinking, "Oh, that sounds like *me*!"

Beyond Positive Thinking reflects what I have learned during my own miraculous healing. It contains the wisdom of men and women like you with whom I have discussed these mind techniques while helping them to achieve inner peace and their unspoken dreams. So you see, this book is not only the result of study and research; more importantly, it arises from the hopes, fears, happiness, and pain of daily life. The mind techniques presented in *Beyond Positive Thinking* are centuries old—so simple that they have been ignored. They are neither time-consuming nor difficult. By using these techniques, you can replace your anxiety, tension, sickness, and failure with peace, harmony, health, and success.

I am especially grateful to my students, who are too numerous to mention individually, for their support and friendship. Without their assistance and inspiration, this book could not have been written. One of those students, Maureen Kovich, provided the financial backing for the preparation of this book. I also thank Clare Wulker, who assisted me in preparing the manuscript for publication.

I am deeply grateful to members of my family for their love and support: to my sisters Mary Lou Diener and Wanda Smith for sharing their lives with me; to my son-in-law Jim Steinkamp for his encouragement; to my grandmother Mary Tabor for her inspiration and encouragement; to my mother, Gladys Wuebbling, for her love, discipline, and right guidance; and to my stepfather, Frank Wuebbling, for his patience.

ONE

Become a New Creation

You are in charge of your life—your *ideas* are. Why not take charge today? By channeling the power of your ideas, you can change your life. Throughout history, the wisdom of Victor Hugo's statement "An invasion of armies can be resisted, but not an idea whose time has come" has been proven. In Russia, Vladimir Lenin defeated a mighty army with his pen, enslaving millions of people with the power of his ideas. Decades later, in the United States, Martin Luther King, Jr.'s, ideas spearheaded the civil rights movement that freed millions of people—another idea whose time had come.

Your time has come. Today. Well-known historical figures are not the only ones with ideas that can change lives. Your ideas spring from the same source that Lenin and King tapped. Now is the time to recognize the tremendous power of your own ideas and fully appreciate their power to change your life. In the following chapters, I will show you how your ideas can draw those things you desire to yourself and how you can stop attracting the conditions that are limiting your life. This method is far beyond positive thinking and mind power because its spiritual orientation encompasses your whole life.

FROM HOPELESSNESS TO HOPE

Do you think that nothing can help you, that you've read all the self-help books and seen counselors, and nothing made any difference—that you are really hopeless? I, too, have been to the point of hopelessness, and I don't want to see anyone else there. That is why I have written this book.

Ten years ago, when I was an office manager, my world began to fall apart. As my rheumatoid arthritis became worse, I was unable to work and barely able to support my three children. My husband had abandoned us; with no child support, I was forced to apply for welfare. I was so crippled that when I walked upstairs, my children had to push me up. If I wanted to uncap the cooking oil, I waited until one of the children came home from school to do it for me. I lived in constant pain. The only future I could see was in a wheelchair, remaining on welfare. I felt worthless, hopeless in body and spirit.

Then a friend gave me *The Power of Your Subconscious Mind*, by Dr. Joseph Murphy.* In Murphy's book I learned that our thoughts are things and whatever we think and send out into the universe will manifest in our lives. This concept opened the doors of freedom for me. I began a search that has been continuous. The motivation for my search was nothing subtle such as intellectual curiosity or spiritual hunger because at this time, when my life was filled with pain, I did not know that I was missing either one. While seeking relief from pain, I found a mind technique that worked; the more I read about the immense power of thoughts and ideas, and how they could play a role in my life, the more excited I became.

Two or three times each day I would affirm, "My body is perfect and whole; every cell is perfect and whole; every bone is perfect and whole." Notice that I said my body *is*, not my body

---

*Joseph Murphy, *The Power of Your Subconscious Mind* (Englewood Cliffs, N.J.: Prentice-Hall, Inc., 1963).

will be. I also used visualization; for thirty-four seconds, I pictured myself as well and whole—as I was at another time in my life. I would feel that experience and remember how it felt to feel good; each day I meditated for thirty minutes. After six months, my body started to respond to the ideas I gave it. My mind, my world, and my life began to take on a new truth, a new beginning.

Like Dr. Murphy, I experienced a complete healing. Because of this, I have dedicated my life to teaching others what I have learned through my experiences and study. At first, I held self-development classes in my home; then I opened a nonprofit healing/counseling center for the sick and hopeless called the *House of HOPE. HOPE* is an abbreviation for Help Other People Evolve; this is our purpose. The principles we use are different from those of medical clinics. Medical doctors assume a leadership role; they tell sick people what to do in order to feel better, and the patients in turn become passive recipients. At my center there are no doctors and there are no patients. We are all teachers who teach one another. After you read Chapter 4, you will understand why we are all teachers.

My HOPE center was started from selfish motives; all the volunteers and I were being healed by helping to heal others. We were not there to change other people but to find some sense of inner peace for ourselves by learning to give.

We found ourselves surrounded by a culture that places great emphasis on possessing, competition, and fear. Fortunately, increasingly more people seem to be awakening to an inner consciousness that says perhaps there is another way: Maybe there is a way of learning how to give without expecting anything in return. Maybe we can truly *accept* another person rather than try to *change* that person. The future and past are irrelevant; the only time is now.

This book is my effort to share my message of inner peace with more people than I could reach through my clinic. First of all, in this chapter, I am going to describe for you some of the techniques I have used and taught others to use to change their lives. You will be able to use these techniques immediately, even before you finish reading the other chapters to find out why these techniques work.

Chapter 2 describes the laws of the Infinite Intelligence as I have learned them in the Bible and explains how these laws relate to our lives. In Chapter 3, I discuss the conscious and subconscious minds and the Superior Intelligence, explaining how these minds interact to guide us.

Chapter 4 discusses the power of love in your life: love for yourself, your Higher Self, your spouse, and everyone else. In Chapter 5, you will learn how to set goals for yourself, to find and fulfill your hidden potential, and to make full use of your imagination.

Chapter 6 explains the essential principle of releasing—letting go—and letting the Supreme Intelligence rule, and it stresses the importance of recognizing lessons in our lives. We short-circuit our powers when we retain negative thoughts, and we run in circles when we do not recognize the lessons of life. Chapter 7 discusses how to pray and the importance of prayer in your life.

Chapter 8 describes meditation in detail; I recommend that everyone meditate for thirty minutes a day. Chapter 9 contains a healing prayer that you should recite before proclaiming any new affirmations as well as affirmations you use in many situations. The last chapter contains a list of books I have found to be very helpful.

BEYOND POSITIVE THINKING

Now that you know the direction of this book, it is time to begin your journey toward inner peace. If after reading about the techniques in this chapter you have a difficult time feeling positive about what you are affirming and visualizing, you most likely harbor negative attitudes. You pity yourself, show suspicion, criticize, and have an inferiority complex. Your personality is pessimistic. You are inconsiderate, cruel, and rude. You reap worry, tension, stress, sickness, and failure.

Negative personalities . . .
- are filled with fear, hate, and doubt
- are inconsiderate, cruel, cold, rude, pessimistic, weak, drab, irritable, and sour
- possess frustration, tension, despondency, worry, sickness, fatigue, loneliness, boredom, and unhappiness

If the negative personality fits you in any way, erase the words "I can't," "It won't," "I'm not" from your vocabulary. Each time you start to use these words, check yourself. Once you begin thinking positively about yourself, you will become more aware of these negative statements. As soon as you hear yourself saying "I can't do it" or "It just won't work," all you need to say is *"Cancel."* This magic word will erase thoughts in your subconscious.

While I was changing the negative atmosphere in my house to a positive one, I put up signs saying *cancel* throughout the house to help my children and me remember. We were also surrounded by signs proclaiming *I am, I can, I will.* High-traffic areas such as the refrigerator door and the bathroom mirror are ideal places for these signs.

Positive personalities . . .
- are filled with love, faith, and hope
- are cheerful, friendly, enthusiastic, decisive, warm, relaxed, courageous, sincere, and optimistic
- possess love, inner peace, security, happiness, health, success, recognition, energy, and friendship

How will you know when your life is positive? You will possess confidence, belief, and expectations. Your personality will be optimistic, sincere, relaxed, and enthusiastic. Your results will be achievement, health, happiness, love, and growth. You will use the words "I can," "It will," "I will," and "I am." Most importantly, you will have inner peace.

Did you know that:

- scientists have found anxiety to be the emotion most damaging to the stomach because it is linked to the formation of ulcers?

- neurotic female mice are more likely to contract breast cancers than female mice with healthy nervous systems?

- bacteria are more likely to infect people who worry and fret?

- a teenager's frame of mind plays a major role in an acne problem, a problem that can sometimes be alleviated by discussion?

- acute tooth decay may follow severe mental stress?

- an emotional upset may trigger the development of appendicitis?

- asthma has psychological origins and is more a symptom than a disease?

- climate has no influence on allergies, colds, or bronchitis?

These ailments are all matters of tension. Fear, tension, anxiety, and nervousness may all be triggering pain and suffering. Even the *idea* of fear can cause us real physical harm. Remove the negative elements from your life, and better health is yours.

If the idea of fear holds such a powerful influence, just think what the ideas of love, faith, belief, and health can do! Why have the universities that train medical and mental doctors overlooked the power of suggestion in healing our minds and bodies? Medicine, chiropractic, and osteopathy are sciences that treat the body to alleviate disease. They all have a place in healing; yet when the disease is of the mind, all three fail to bring about a cure. These sciences fail because they treat the effects when the real causes are in the mind. Christian Science, psychotherapy, and psychiatry are sciences that treat the mind to alleviate disease. These sciences do cure many people, but they fail to cure

problems of a purely physical origin. Why. . .
in accord with the laws of life and this univ. . .

One way to help guard yourself from phy. . .
to know that what appears to be negative to y. . .
reality, very positive. For example, you may be gett. . .
from worrying about losing your job or whether a bette. . .
be available when you leave your present job. Rememb. . .
some of the happiest moments occur after a period of despa. . .
darkness. Happiness is not always getting everything you wan. . .
Both negative and positive energies are required for a light to
glow; similarly, these factors complement each other in our lives.
Take a step beyond positive thinking and learn to cope with the
negative factors in your life. Don't run from them; *learn* from
them.

When you have a serious problem, ask yourself, "What
possible action can I take right now? Can I change the problem?
Can I eliminate it?" If you cannot eliminate the problem, then
adapt to it. By changing your attitude toward the problem, and
by getting your mind to change its thinking, you will prevent
your mental fears from damaging your body. Whenever you start
to experience fear concerning a problem, conjure up strong faith
instead in order to protect your body. You have a choice: You
can emphasize the negative or the positive in any given situation.
This freedom of choice will be discussed more thoroughly in
Chapter 6.

Remember the last time you prayed hard for something,
and even thought positively about it, and you didn't receive it?
The reason you did not get your desire rests in the difference
between two words: *hallucination* and *image*. A *hallucination* is any
false or mistaken idea, a delusion. An *image* is a mental picture,
a sculptured likeness, to mirror, reflect, and project. Positive
thinking, and even prayer, cannot produce the desired results
when the image you hold is not the same image held by the
Infinite Intelligence and it is not for your good. For example, it
could be that you are praying that a strikingly attractive person
you see on the bus every day will fall madly in love with you.

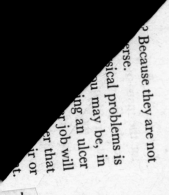

...wly poisoning his or her spouse
...a gruesome example, but you
...lucination instead of an image.
...hallucinations.

...demonstrates the difference
...One day a man saw his wife
...b. He said, "Honey, why are

...lways did it."

...siting his mother-in-law, he
asked ...e end of the leg of lamb like
that?"

Sl... ..., ...y mother always did it that way."

Several months later, he met grandma and said, "Grandma, why do you cut the end of the leg of lamb off that way?"

She said, "Sonny, I have a pan only this big," and she brought out a very small pan. That was her reason for cutting the leg of lamb off. Generation to generation had acquired a cooking tradition based on hallucination, not image.

TECHNIQUES FOR POSITIVE THINKING

Affirmation Technique. The word *affirm* means *to make firm, to make positive.* If you recite a particular affirmation for twenty-two consecutive days, your subconscious mind will react positively to what you are saying. Then whatever you desire will manifest itself in your life. Say the affirmation for three or four minutes three times each day and actually feel what you are affirming.

A Healing Prayer. Before you begin using the affirmation technique described in the preceding paragraph, say the following healing prayer:

> *O Higher Self, You who read all of my thoughts and know me and every detail of my consciousness. Examine me now and know my heart; walk*

back with me through all the darkened areas of my life and shed light into all of the areas that are still in darkness. I ask to be reborn at this moment, this day. I ask that You heal all the sufferings that I might have experienced during those times of growing up. Erase all of the negatives from my being and allow me to know that I am truly loved by You. Fill me with a sense of Your purpose and of Your love. As I begin my affirmations on this day, I ask that Your blessings be upon them. I thank You because everything I am, I am in You. I am deserving of what I am asking You for. I rest in You and thank You, for I know that it is being done. Amen.

Whether you select an affirmation from Chapter 9 or write one of your own, start saying it daily. Do not just repeat this affirmation mindlessly, but actually form a feeling within yourself that this is a truth, that it is a fact. Decree it is so and it will manifest in your life. Job said, "Thou shalt also decree a thing, and it shall be established unto thee; and the light shall shine upon thy ways."

If you are ill, you may want to affirm, "I am perfect, I am whole, I am healthy." Remember that to affirm is to state that it is so; you must also *feel* that it is so. As you state the affirmation, your subconscious mind is receiving the affirmation. The subconscious mind does not judge; it accepts that the statement must be so. The wonderful thing about the subconscious mind is its ability to make things happen.

Sixteen steps to better health

1. Stop complaining about your aches and pains.

2. Read books about other people's healing experiences.

3. Watch your diet.

4. Begin physical exercise.

5. Follow your doctor's orders.

6. See a nutritionist.

7. Lead a balanced life: Work, play, and rest.

8. Enjoy fresh air each day.

. Make a prayer wheel concerning your illness.

10. Decree that better health is yours.

11. Say affirmations.

12. Picture yourself as a well person.

13. Praise your body.

14. Release the negative influences in your life.

15. Give thanks for your renewed health.

Your subconscious mind loves to give you what you ask for; if you command it, your subconscious must fulfill your order. For example, if you tell your subconscious mind, "My bank account is overflowing; I have all the money in the world to pay my bills and buy all that I need and more," your subconscious takes action by making things happen in your life so that what you requested will be manifested. You may, for example, find a job paying a higher salary; or, someone who owes you money may send you a check; you may find a part-time job or discover free-lance opportunities. You will see the flow continue as long as you affirm this desire, stating that it is so.

You may find that, despite repeated daily affirmations, your desires do not manifest. Remember that your affirmation succeeds when you do not have a mental conflict or disagreement with yourself. Prayers or affirmations will fail to manifest if an idea, a concept, or a suggestion does not seem logical to your conscious mind before it lodges into your subconscious mind. You must believe the words you proclaim to be true. If you don't believe that you're going to get a particular job and you continue affirming with fear in your heart, "The job is mine; I'm worthy to have it," you won't get it. The secret is that the subconscious mind doesn't become impressed with words, but, rather, with *feelings*. Therefore, if you say, "I'm courageous," but you feel frightened, you will manifest the message of fear in your body, your mind, and your life. A good affirmation to start with that will not create any conflict in you is, "By day and night I am

10

being prospered in all of my interests." This affirmation will not arouse any arguments in your conscious mind.

Too frequently we overlook a great power called *imagination*. You use imagination in a negative way when you worry about something that hasn't happened; for example, fearing an upcoming examination or an airplane flight. This type of imagination can be as real as if you were experiencing the actual happening. Take a good look at your everyday life; have you been using negative imagination? Remember that today you reap the thoughts that you programmed into your subconscious mind as truths yesterday.

Visualization Technique. This technique uses positive imagination. Sit down in a chair and relax. Become as limp as a Raggedy Ann or Andy doll. Loosen your tight clothing such as belts, ties, skirt, or slacks. Take your shoes off and keep your feet flat on the floor. Then close your eyes and picture in your mind what you have been affirming.

If you can hold an image for thirty-four seconds, the image will sink into your subconscious and manifest itself in your life. For example, imagine yourself lining up six lemons on a table, and then cutting each lemon in two. Hold each half between your fingers and suck out the seeds; then spit the seeds out. Allow the lemon juice to flow down your throat and experience the flow of juices in your mouth. Got the picture? What happened to your thoughts? You were able to produce a strong feeling. This is the kind of image that can change your life.

Now activate the strong mental picture of something you want—perhaps a condition or trait that requires development. Add feelings to the picture being held. Thinking "money" won't give you money, even if you see 100-dollar bills. Feeling that you already have the money will bring you the desired results. Imagine how you would feel after you receive the money. See yourself putting the extra money in a savings account.

Then, take action. Act as though you already have the money. Continue concentrating on how it will feel to pay your bills. Do not allow your thoughts to waiver. You must devise a plan to help you accomplish your image—this could be looking for a new job or seeking work in addition to your full-time job. Along with this action, hold the thought that your present job is wonderful and pays you a fine salary.

In *The Power of Your Subconscious Mind*, Dr. Murphy provides an effective example of how affirmations can help you accomplish tasks such as selling your house.* The first thing you would do in order to sell your house is to affirm, "My house is sold; it is exactly what the buyers want and the price is right." Then start visualizing. In your mind's eye, see your house with a "For Sale" sign in front of it. Then see a "Sold" sign replace the "For Sale" sign; picture a check in the amount that you want for your house. Naturally, the price you are asking should be a fair price; if it is not, you will not feel truth within your heart and your subconscious mind will not bring it forth.

See the prospective buyers looking at the house and liking it. See the check being extended to your hand and look at the amount. Then see yourself spending the money and buying whatever it is that you want. If you are putting the money into a savings account, picture that transaction.

Another thing that you must keep in mind is to talk positively about the house. Don't say to yourself, "Oh, this house—who would want this old dilapidated thing?" or, "I'm so tired of it; nobody else would want it." If you say that, you provide a barrier to the house's being sold. Instead, say, "There is someone who is ready to buy my house at this very moment who will love it. It will be perfect for him." This will not be hard to believe if you recall *your* first apartment; maybe it was only one room, but you loved it because it was your home. It's the same feeling that somebody else is going to experience about your house.

Sleep Technique. Before you go to sleep each night, when you are in a drowsy state and very relaxed, say your affirmation and

---

*Joseph Murphy, *The Power of Your Subconscious Mind* (Englewood Cliffs, N.J.: Prentice-Hall, Inc., 1963).

visualize what you desire, then go to sleep. You will ke
you have affirmed and visualized in your subconscious
night. It will be there in your body working, sending its messag̃ᵉ
out into the universe. When you awake in the morning, before
you get out of bed, restate your affirmation and visualize what
you desire; experience the feeling.

Weeding Technique.   Use this technique at night before you go to
sleep. Pretend that your mind is a garden. (As you know, whatever
you sow in your garden you will reap.) Pluck out of your mind
all the negatives that have sprung up throughout the day: the
hate, resentment, hurt, mistreatment, and so on. Pluck out all
of the "weeds" and start to feed your "garden" positive
affirmations such as, "I am perfect, I am whole, I am a child
of the Supreme Intelligence," or any other positive ideas that
you want to put back into your body. In the morning, as you
jump out of bed, remember to say, "Thank you, God, for a lovely
day," and it will be.

Take-Charge Technique.   This technique is just as effective as it
is uncomplicated. Repeat ninety-nine times each day for a week:
"I am master of my fate mentally, physically, and spiritually."

RECAPTURE CHILDLIKE FEELINGS

Remember when your childish faith told you that you would
receive something for Christmas? When I was young, my friends
and I would turn cartwheels, confident that whoever turned the
best cartwheel would get her wish. I also remember looking to
the sky and saying, "Twinkle, twinkle, little star . . ." and wishing
upon a star. When we spotted the brightest star, we believed
that we were going to get our wishes.

   As we mature, we lose the feeling of being one with all life
and the accompanying fantasy when we learn that the stars are
planets, only distant gaseous bodies. Bombarded with negative

programming by our failures, we become enslaved by ideas that keep us from experiencing a fuller, richer expression of life. Try to recapture that childlike feeling of being all powerful and know that you can create your heaven here and now. Remember, you have a choice. By having faith in yourself and your Higher Self within, you can change your life.

Believe, imagine, and you become. Some well-known sports figures, including golfer Ben Hogan, have found that imaginal practice sharpens their skills as much as physical practice. They imagine themselves practicing perfect golf swings, making baskets, and hitting home runs while sitting in their armchairs. And it works because they *believe* it will work.

A POSITIVE-THINKING FABLE

Once upon a time, Mr. Chin opened a small store in suburban America. He lived above the store with his family. He sent his children to school and introduced himself to all of his neighbors. Gradually, the Chin family became the object of prejudice. Some of the neighbors wrote "Go home Chinks" on their windows; one by one, the other stores on the block became vacant. The people surrounding the Chinese family moved out of the neighborhood.

Then one day a large department store chain began buying up the empty stores. When store representatives tried to talk Mr. Chin into selling, he said that he would not be bought out. Patiently, the representatives, called the Community Continuity Coordinators, explained to Mr. Chin that large department stores buy in such large quantities that they would be able to undersell any small competitors in stores like Mr. Chin's. The representatives guaranteed him that he would not make any money and urged him to sell, but Mr. Chin stood his ground.

The large department store chain began remodeling the stores on both sides of Mr. Chin. On the day before the grand opening, workmen erected banners proclaiming "Grand Opening" on the stores to the left and to the right of Mr. Chin's store.

Early the next morning, before the grand opening, Mr. Chin climbed a ladder and placed a sign above the door to his store: It read, "Entrance Here."

Now *that's* a positive thinker!

VISUALIZE AND BELIEVE

I once wanted a new car, so I began programming my subconscious for it. I believed I would get it, I imagined how it would look, and I got it. Whenever people asked me what type of car I wanted, I told them. When I would drive through parking lots with my daughter, I would say, "Well, there's my car," and she would ask, "Mother, what color are you going to get?" I would answer, "A white one—that's the color I want." Then one evening I was taken out to dinner by a couple as a token of their appreciation. Twice when she was seriously ill I had diagnosed the wife's ailments, even though doctors had failed to do so. During the evening I was talking about the power of visualizing and believing and mentioned that I was programming for a special car. He mentioned that he wanted to sell his car, which happened to be the same type of car I was programming for. He looked at me and said, "Patricia, if you pay off my loan, the car is yours." That meant that I received a $19,000 car for $7,000!

Another time that visualizing and believing worked for me was when I wanted to appear on a popular television show in our area. While I was being interviewed by a newspaper reporter, I said, "I'm going to be on Bob Braun's show soon." The reporter wrote about it long before I was asked to be on that show; later I became a regular guest. My belief had made it so.

Before you can believe like this, you must believe that you are worthy of all the wonderful things your Higher Self intends for you to have. Frequently, religious beliefs get in the way of our feeling good about ourselves. I am going to explore some of these negative ideas in the next chapter.

TWO

Discover the Laws of the Supreme Intelligence

After Karl Marx described religion as the opiate of the people, Miguel de Unamuno added, "Let us give them opium so that they can sleep and dream." Too often, religious practices are equated with this type of dreamy passivity, a bland ritual you outgrow with Sunday school. Religion's vibrant message, God's love for His children, has been lost. As a result, millions of men and women today are morally and spiritually uncertain, not quite sure of where they are going, or what to believe in, or why. This uncertainty produces fear, and fear smothers the creativity that is in each of them. The consequence is a host of perplexed people living strained lives rooted in a vague sense of restless insecurity.

If only each of them could stand and look up to the starry heavens, to discover the source of everything happening in this universe. God instructed us to, "Lift up your eyes on high and behold who hath created these things." As you look upward, you cannot help but wonder with spellbound fascination at the stars, those distant whispers of light that come from somewhere so far away that only telescopes can reveal their origin.

After looking up, observe the earth's graceful, twenty-four-hour rotation, suspended in space. It moves with perfect precision. Job said of the Infinite Intelligence, "He hangeth the earth upon nothing." Could such clocklike precision, balance, and harmony be the result of blind chance, chaos, or cosmic accident? No. This vast space, this place in which we live, was not created by accident. We are not specks of cosmic dust in a chaotic universe with no purpose or design. We are children of the Infinite Intelligence, the Creator of all.

When we look up to the heavens, to the stars, we stand in awe. To think that as large as each star is, and as small as we are, we are the astronomers! People will always be able to study and appreciate the stars, to do what a star cannot do—to think. Wouldn't this be a good time and place to set our thinking straight about the Infinite Intelligence?

This chapter was written for persons of all religious beliefs; it is not meant to separate Christian readers from those readers who hold other beliefs. Throughout this book, I have used the words *God, Supreme Intelligence, Infinite Intelligence,* and *Higher Self* interchangeably. My message is one of unity, light, and love for all humanity. Whether you believe in Jesus Christ or not, I believe that your deity also brought the same message of hope to you. So, no matter what your religious beliefs are, please continue reading; keep what you feel comfortable with, and discard the rest.

YOUR HIGHER SELF

Were you startled by my statement that your religious beliefs do not matter, that my message is for everyone? This is true because the Higher Self within you is the essence of humanity; It is the real source of your wisdom, your basic will to live, and your healing love. Your Higher Self is the impelling force behind your most noble acts, your tenderest moments, and your best insights. Your Higher Self existed long before your body or personality came into being. Quite simply, It is the presence of the Supreme Being within. Your Higher Self lives in the heavenly realm of wisdom, talent, strength, and love. Possessing all things, It does not owe Its existence to your physical body or anything on the physical plane. Your Higher Self stands ready to serve as a true parent to you.

Numerous stories have described the miraculous transformations that occur when the personality, body, and Higher Self come together. Although abstract and intangible, your Higher Self is certainly not unknowable. For those of you who have not experienced the reality of the Higher Self, I suggest that you establish this contact through meditative discipline, as described in Chapter 8. When you seek to make contact with your Higher Self, you make contact with the Supreme Source—the God within all of us. Once you make contact with your Higher Self through meditation, you will never again feel unguided, unloved, or empty. Most people find the concept of an indwelling Presence difficult to grasp because they have always prayed to a God they imagine to be sitting on a cloud-bedecked throne somewhere in heaven. At times, this distant Presence seems to be hiding, unreachable; this is why we needed Jesus Christ and the other prophets to guide us back to the Higher Self within.

THE TEACHINGS OF JESUS CHRIST

Many people say that Jesus Christ is the Savior of the earth. Some say that He was a great prophet, a teacher, and others have said that He was a fanatic who ended up in failure and ruin after a short public career. Whatever you call Him doesn't matter; what *is* important is that Jesus Christ has influenced so many people's lives by His doctrine, or at least by the doctrine that has been attributed to Him. Jesus has become a religious inspiration throughout the world.

Has Christianity really expressed what Jesus stood for as a man, what He taught and left for us, what He really wished for us to believe? If Jesus were here today, would He be pleased with the teachings of His brothers and their interpretation of His Word? I am not sure He would be pleased, because today some religious leaders become entangled in details while they

19

overlook the principles. You will find in the scriptures that Jesus taught only basic principles. He knew that when the spirit is right, the details take care of themselves.

Jesus brought us truth, and in that truth He brought a practical method for the development of our souls and the shaping of our lives and destinies. In Jesus's teaching, you will find, as I have, an explanation of the true nature of God. Jesus explains why we make mistakes and the reason why each of us becomes sick. He gives us the meaning of life and death and tells how to overcome obstacles and temptations. He shows us how we can bring health, prosperity, and true happiness into our lives, the lives of those we love, and those with whom we share this universe.

Read this chapter with an open mind. Put aside any recollection of religious upbringing and things you have been taught. Share with me the Word that I believe Christ brought to each of us on this earth.

At the lowest time in my life, when there was nowhere to turn, I started to reach for the Supreme Intelligence. Turning to guidance and council like so many other depressed people, I opened the Bible and started to read the New Testament. I believe that I was healed of my crippled condition by the power of the Word and the mind techniques that became part of my daily life.

The God that I have come to know so well in the last few years teaches that we are punished only for our own mistakes. For example, if I purchase a house which burns down two months later, this is not God's doing. I made the mistake of not having the electrical wiring checked before buying. This is a human error, not divine punishment. God also says that no matter how bad we are, He, as our loving father, will forgive us. Best of all, He will forgive us as soon as we ask for forgiveness and as many times as we ask to be forgiven.

Heaven is all around us. It is not a place far off in the skies that we have to wait to reach someday. You can reach it now. All you have to do is recognize that heaven is the presence of your Higher Self; it is the inner peace that you feel. Heaven is a mind that is not in torment—there is no aging, no decaying; it is the renewing of the spirit, knowing the truth, and being able to experience the infinite freedom and perfect bliss of where you are in the present.

Have you ever been told that it is blessed to be persecuted as the result of your right thinking because the prophets and the saints were persecuted? Do not believe it. Experiencing persecution is not the will of the Supreme Intelligence. Rather, that will is joy and peace, love and harmony. The Higher Self does not oversee anyone's persecution. We persecute ourselves whenever we give way to fear, despondency, and anger in our daily lives. There is no virtue in being persecuted. You will learn as I have that what you experience in your own life is your own doing, not the result of someone persecuting you. If you are being persecuted, then look within yourself, because that is where the persecution originates.

Jesus was not a martyr when He went to the cross. At any time He could have avoided the crucifixion, but He knew that it was necessary to die in order to demonstrate His love for us. Christ chose to do this for us in His own way; He was not martyred. So there is no great beauty nor virtue in martyrdom. There have been a lot of martyrs through the ages—wonderful people who have experienced self-sacrifice: This is a spiritual truth. But if you have been persuaded into being a martyr, you are going to bring a great deal of unnecessary havoc and pain to yourself. God is not asking you to martyr yourself for Him. Remember that your Higher Self is love, beauty, truth, and goodness.

MIRACLES STILL HAPPEN

Some of you will be very uneasy when I discuss miracles because you have been taught that there are no such things. I have talked to people who became embarrassed when miracles were mentioned and refused to discuss them. They did not even want to know where to find passages about miracles in the Bible because their ministers had explained away all of the miracles Jesus had performed. Some ministers do acknowledge a few selected miracles and then refuse to discuss the rest.

Did the miracles really happen? Did Jesus really perform them? If we conclude that miracles did not happen, then the rest of the gospel story loses all real truth. If Jesus did not perform the miracles and did things only for the sake of display, then the New Testament is devoid of all significance. Turn to the New Testament and read the truth in the four gospels and you will agree that these miracles actually happened. John states that Jesus said, "The works that I do shall he do also; and greater works than these shall I do." Yet some religious and spiritual leaders today do not believe that people have the right to perform miracles because only Jesus could cure the blind and the lame.

Do we see miracles today? Yes, we do! For example, a doctor tells a child's parents that the child will die without having a particular operation performed before the end of the week. The parents pray with this child and before the operation can be performed, the child recovers. That child was healed through the parents' prayers. Another example is the miracles in the lives of recipients of organs donated by the family of an accident victim. Whenever we touch the definite higher law in this universe and know how to work with it, this law manifests wonderful things in our lives.

When you learn to pray as the healed child's parents prayed, you will find that prayer can create miracles in your life. (Be sure to read Chapters 7 and 9 about prayer and affirmations.) Once you learn the art of praying as it was taught by that great teacher, Jesus, you will find that you are performing many miracles every day in your own life.

Jesus performed the miracles that you read about in the Bible so that you would be able to perform those same miracles to overcome sickness, mistakes, and limitations in your own life.

When your mind is open, you receive spiritual truth from the great book of life. Under divine inspiration, this spiritual truth brings divine wisdom to those who have integrated spiritual knowledge into their lives. You will learn that you have dominion over all things; one of the most important is your own mind. You will learn that you have a free will and, specifically, that free will should be part of your thinking process. Also, you will find that your desires create your world. Look around at your surroundings and realize that where you live and what is happening in your life have been chosen by you. At this particular time of your life, you are reaping whatever you have sown.

KEEP AN OPEN MIND

I will not ask any of you to accept this truth concerning positive thinking at this moment because I know that people must prove things to themselves first. You probably would not have picked up this book unless deep inside your heart you had a desire to change things in yourself or your life. Each of us has a great need for better health, peace of mind, and spiritual development; the techniques in this book will help you to experience them in your life. The task, however, is not an easy one; I have been working at this for the last ten years. I still have to work to accomplish the inner peace I feel within myself each day.

If you are prepared to break away from old ideas, old concepts, and old thoughts, then continue with me. Keep your mind open and you will find that the price you pay will be well worth it. Those of you who are reading this book in perfect health, please continue reading so that your health will remain perfect. Those of you who have financial worth and are prosperous, look to God the giver, and not at your gift, and you will continue to be prosperous. Be certain that you share unselfishly with others as the Supreme Intelligence has shared with you.

GOD THE FATHER

When I reached for the Bible after reading Dr. Murphy's book, *The Power of Your Subconscious Mind*, I read with an open mind and an open heart.* I discovered that my relationship with God is that of a parent and child. Suddenly the words of the New Testament flooded my heart. When I read the Lord's Prayer, God became a living father to me. I became His child, and because of that, I became important. I read and reread that part of the Bible until it seeped into my heart and soul, enabling me to remove from my consciousness those erroneous ideas about God I had learned in childhood.

In the New Testament, I found that I was the offspring of God, the Supreme Intelligence who gives us life and breath. The Supreme Intelligence gave us life so that we would reach out to the Higher Self and find peace and love, for in the Higher Self we live, move, and have our being.

CHILDREN OF GOD

Like Christ, you have the right to your Father's estate. Whatever the Father has, you inherit. As soon as you have the spiritual wisdom to understand this great truth, you can claim your rights and obtain them. You are not a servant—you are a child of the Infinite Intelligence. Know that your Father who loves you very much wishes you to inherit good health, much beauty, and even more joy. His thoughts are your thoughts. He'll give all these gifts to you; all that you must do is ask for them.

Our Father has given us dominion over all things. So claim them, accept them, know that you have a right to them. Because the Supreme Intelligence knew that you would be afraid, Matthew teaches, "Ask, and it shall be given you; seek, and ye shall

*Joseph Murphy, *The Power of Your Subconscious Mind* (Englewood Cliffs, N.J.: Prentice-Hall, Inc., 1963).

find; knock and it shall be opened unto you." N
not said, "I'll give you half." He gives you the
all of it. Claim it as your own. Ask yourself i
He said; if He did, then you have the righ
you will receive.

Remove yourself from mental, physical, and
dage; stop being a slave of your habits, of your thinki
yesterday. Start today to see the truth. Know right now that
your ill health, or poverty, or unhappiness is not the will of your
Higher Self. God's very name means to be holy. Anything holy
cannot send troubles, sickness, or death because that is not its
nature. Know that with all your heart. Through your Higher
Self your Father loves you; He is joy, harmony, success, love,
and kindness. If you believe that you are a child of the Supreme
Intelligence, refuse to accept anything less than success, happiness, peace, joy, contentment, and love.

Start Today.   Start today by praying, meditating, and reorganizing
your life so that you rid yourself of old habits, old thoughts, old
concepts, and old ideas. Fill your being with positive energy and
positive thoughts, and claim your freedom. Claim your Father,
and inherit the things that are His. In order to prosper from the
principles that the Infinite Intelligence gave us, be strong, and
keep working at them. Believe. Otherwise, the principles will not
manifest in your life.

If you do believe, and use all of your willpower, you will
start to experience perfect health, prosperity, happiness, and
energy galore. Your body will no longer be burdened with daily
worries; you will feel wonderful, and because of your enthusiasm,
people will love to be near you.

YOU ARE YOUR OWN GUIDE

Even though some ministers and gurus are very charismatic, do
not put any of them on pedestals. Follow the Higher Self within
you; your Higher Self must be your guide. Certainly, you should

from the teachings of churches and attend workshops and
ures to broaden your understanding. Talk to other people
nd learn all you can, but do not surrender your spiritual judgment to them. You owe your spiritual integrity to your indwelling
Higher Self and no one else. I hope that you will use this book
as a stepping stone to spiritual wisdom. It should never become
a bedrock of belief. You must be free to move on, to decide your
own spiritual growth for yourself.

The Supreme Intelligence has not created Greeks, or Jews,
or Protestants as the chosen ones because there is no chosen race
or religion. No group of human beings is spiritually superior to
any other. We have all received equal partnerships in the Higher
Self. Because of this, no one has the authority to decide what is
right or wrong for you. Something within yourself should give
you the truth.

Seek the Truth. How do you know which religion is the right
religion? How do you know which truth is the right truth? Which
teacher is the right teacher? One of the tests for finding the truth
for yourself is to ask, "Does what they are saying to me work in
my life today?" Remember, the truth always works. Truth heals.
It purifies the soul. It releases pain in your life. Persons working
with truth will be able to lay their hands on the sick, and the
sick shall recover. By their fruits ye shall know them. When they
demonstrate something, it will come to pass.

Observe the conditions of the minister's life. Remember,
"As within, so without." You can tell where a minister is standing
spiritually by looking at his environment and his appearance.
Everything in the soul is reflected in the outer body sooner or
later. Also, everything in a person's outer world eventually
manifests in some way in the inner being.

Live the Truth. Learn to look to your Higher Self as your source;
look to It for your needs and all things will be given to you. If
you look to your spouse or friends to fulfill all your needs, you
will be disillusioned. People can fail you, but your Higher Self

will not. For example, you may feel very secure in your job. But if your employer loses his business, where will you be if all of your faith is in him? If you had placed your faith in your Higher Self, you could be confident that you would soon have another job.

Some people seem to grow more cynical as they grow older. And it is no wonder. Each time they placed all their faith in elected officials or religious leaders to solve the world's problems or their own personal problems, they were disappointed. If they had placed all their faith in the Higher Self, they would be just as old but a lot happier.

If you experience discouragement because of your own sense of unworthiness while you are seeking spiritual wisdom, turn to the Supreme Source. Your Higher Self will see that you attract those situations and people in your life that you need. Remember, the kingdom of God is within, and you need only ask to receive.

Jesus said, "Know the truth and the truth shall make you free." He spent all of His life instructing people about truth. In your search for the truth, you are the master of your inner kingdom, possessing the power to accept or reject thoughts. One way to become more free is to take full charge of yourself—to accept the consequences of your thoughts in your life. To help you do this, the next chapter will explain how your conscious and subconscious minds and the Superior Intelligence interact to bring about various circumstances in your life.

THREE

Renewing the Minds
We Possess and Share

Brainpower. We hear about it all the time. But what do we hear about *mindpower*? Nothing. Scientists' discoveries about the functions of the left and right sides of the human brain have been described in many recent books. Unfortunately, not many books have been written about the powers of the conscious and subconscious minds we each possess or the powers of the Superior Intelligence that we share. In this chapter, you will learn how to tap these amazing powers. You will learn how to convey ideas to the subconscious mind by repetition, faith, and expectancy. First, we will look briefly at the brain as the organ of thought.

THE BRAIN

The brain is that portion of your central nervous system in the vertebrate cranium responsible for the interpretation of sensory impulses, the coordination and control of bodily activities, and the exercise of emotions and thought. Scientists have found that the left side of your brain generates logical thoughts; its thinking is linear, organizational, and verbal; it controls the right side of the body. The right side of the brain is a mirror image of the left; it produces intuitive, nonrational, nonverbal, holistic thoughts, and controls the left side of the body.

As the organ of thought, your brain molds you into what you are going to become, what you are, and what you were. In fact, you could be called a *biocomputer*: You are alive and can be programmed or deprogrammed.

Deprogramming will become an important part of your life as you read this book. From the very moment that you were born, everything that you experienced has been recorded within your brain. Messages from your parents, your ministers, the news media, your teachers, and even the traffic cop in the street have all made their impressions in your memory. Your memory registers experiences with your friends and everyone with whom you have been associated. Every experience has programmed your present thinking patterns. These experiences have not all been positive—our world is filled with criticism, cynicism, and negative remarks. These negative impressions are so damaging that they must be deprogrammed. If anyone tries to feed you negativity, do not allow that negativity to impress your consciousness so that it can become part of memory. Think positive thoughts instead. In Chapter 4, I will describe a white-cross technique that you can use to alter negative people's attitudes toward you.

The Conscious Mind. Your brain is in your head; your mind is not. Your mind is an outside force that powers the organ known as your brain. Your conscious mind is reading this book at this very moment, taking in the information that you have read, and storing all this information away in the subconscious mind. This same conscious mind decided what clothing you were going to put on this morning and whether to ask a friend to have lunch today.

The Subconscious Mind. Your subconscious mind has two duties: first, to maintain your bodily functions, to keep your hair growing, your heart beating, and your blood flowing. All of this is taken care of automatically. The second function of your subconscious mind is to store away for future reference any information that you give it. Anything that you have ever done or read is stored in this area. Every time you have been impressed by something you have felt, tasted, smelled, touched, heard, or saw, it was recorded in the subconscious. To illustrate this process, imagine that after an impression is processed by your conscious mind, it passes through a little window to be filed away in your subconscious. Most importantly, the information that has been so carefully filed away is not brought back from your subconscious mind unless you ask for it.

Your subconscious is more than a very powerful information center. Using its storehouse of information, your subconscious sees that you get whatever you demand—it takes you at your word. Tell it "I can't afford it," and your subconscious mind will see to it that you do not have the money to buy what you want. Tell it "I can't do this stupid thing," and your subconscious mind will imobilize your creativity so that you do not have the ability to do whatever you told it you could not do. But if you affirm, "I can do all things through the power of my subconscious mind," you will have all of the money and ability you need.

Change your thoughts and you change your destiny. When thoughts are conveyed to your subconscious mind, impressions are made in your brain cells. As these impressions are made, your subconscious is accepting the ideas and beginning to put them into effect. By associating ideas, your subconscious mind sifts through all of the information you have unknowingly and knowingly assimilated in its effort to put your ideas into motion. As unstoppable as an avalanche, your subconscious enlists the laws of nature and utilizes your infinite power, energy, and wisdom to fulfill your command. Sometimes the solution to your request comes immediately; at other times, it may take longer. It took six months for my subconscious to effect an improvement in my rheumatoid arthritis. To tap these miraculous powers, all you have to do is convey your ideas to your subconscious by repetition, faith, and expectancy.

How to free your subconscious mind
so it can work for you

1. Dismiss all responsibility about the outcome once you have reached a decision about a conscious action. Let your mind run free.

2. Consciously respond to the present moment—make it a habit. By giving all of your attention to the present moment, you will have no time for anxious thoughts about tomorrow. Make long-range plans for tomorrow but don't try to live either tomorrow or yesterday today.

3. Do only one thing at a time.

4. Sleep on it. If you have wrestled with a problem all day without making any apparent progress, dismiss it from your mind. Then sleep on it.

5. Relax while you work. Repeat to yourself several times: "I feel more and more relaxed." Practice this faithfully several times each day.

Your subconscious contains only what you have filed away there (it's not going to do you any good to ask for Burt Reynolds' telephone number or Mohammed Ali's address if you have never known either one). Like your bank account, you can only take out what you put in; you can only recall specific information that you have entered. Just imagine—you can recall at any time any information that you have stored away.

Suppose you and a friend are talking. You say, "Mary, I'm trying to remember the name of that famous restaurant we ate in when we were vacationing in Florida five years ago. It's on the tip of my tongue, but I just can't remember it." So, you change the subject and suddenly you blurt out, "The Diner's Inn—that's it!" In this case, your subconscious was looking through the files under "vacation" and then under "restaurants." Most of us have used this power of recall. Sometimes it takes twenty-four hours or so for the information to come back if your request is sent out into the ethers, into the Superior Intelligence, and it has to filter back into your subconscious mind.

Unfortunately, our subconscious mind does not do much work for us because most of us do not usually ask our subconscious mind for information. We just let our subconscious mind file names, phone numbers, and dates but we rarely ask it to produce. We take memory courses to learn how to remember a telephone number that we call every day, or how to remember a date, while all that we have to do is start using the powers of our subconscious minds.

Once your memory starts serving you, it will not forget. Occasionally, your subconscious will give you wrong information. When it does, your conscious mind will know it and you will send back a second request; the subconscious usually delivers the right information.

Memory Technique. To prove the power of your subconscious mind, try this technique. Think of something in the past—perhaps someone you have not seen since you were a child, someone whose name you cannot remember. Recall the name of a street on which you once lived. All you have to do is to give your subconscious a command in a very positive way, three times. Say aloud, "What was the name of _____? What was the name of _____? What was the name of _____?" Then, just forget it. If the name hasn't come after a few hours, command again, and it will come.

The Superior Intelligence. ESP and creativity originate in the third mind level, the Superior Intelligence. This level is outside your body, in the universe. The Superior Intelligence is the source of sudden inspirations; for example, you are driving along in your car and suddenly you say, "What an idea!" That idea is unrelated to anything you have ever thought before. Or you may think of an idea for an invention that you feel compelled to write down immediately.

The Superior Intelligence is the most important level of the mind because it contains all the answers. These answers are given to writers, artists, psychics, and inventors—anyone who desires to use the Superior Intelligence. This is why two or three inventors in different parts of the world could receive the same information about a perpetual-motion machine or some other energy-saving invention. All of them have received the same idea from the very same source. This is why, when reading two books published simultaneously on the same subject, similar sentences can be found that seem to derive from a common source. These ideas are in the universe.

Because thoughts are in the universe, everyone has an opportunity to reach into that universal consciousness, that Superior Intelligence, that God mind, and bring forward information. The Superior Intelligence contains all the information in the universe—everything you need to know. All you have to do is ask. Most likely, you have already used the Superior Intelligence.

For example, if you could not arrive at a solution to a problem on Thursday evening, you may have said, "Oh, I've got to have that answer by Friday at noon." You go to sleep and wake up Friday morning and, sure enough, the answer comes. It pops into your head and you wonder where it came from, how it happened, how you got the solution. What happened is that your subconscious mind was stumped and sent out a message to the Superior Intelligence, which came up with the answer.

Now you can see why it is so important that you begin using all the powers of your mind and control your negative thoughts so that they do not control you any longer. After you begin to use your inner powers, you will have opened the prison doors of fear and entered into a life described by Paul as that of "the glorious liberty of the children of God."

MAX REPRESENTS MILLIONS

At this point, I'm going to introduce you to Max. Max represents 90 percent of the people in our world. He is full of fear, ill health, frustration, and failure. Each of us has experienced these problems at one time or another. Max is too frustrated to have any motivation in life, too angry to have any goals, and too worrisome to have any expectations. Like millions of others, Max doesn't know that he has the inner power to change his life, to replace ill health with perfect health, frustration with fulfillment, and failure with success.

Remember that whatever your mind dwells on will come into your experience sooner or later. If you dwell on disease, ill health, poverty, strife, or dishonesty, these things will manifest in your life. People claim that they have a right to be angry, and they may honestly think that they do have the right. But is that right worth the consequences of holding these feelings? As we discussed in Chapter 1, whenever you entertain a negative thought, you cause an outer condition to occur from those inner thoughts. Despite the fact that you have a right to be angry, your body will react to these emotions in the form of illness or other limitations in your life.

People like Max are like ships without rudders; they are drifting, waiting for some outside force to blow them in one direction or another. Do not waste the powers of your mind by not using them or by letting your life drift; your mind needs to have a focal point. You need goals. In Chapter 5, I have made some suggestions about how you can begin setting goals for yourself.

MIRACLES HAPPEN EVERY DAY

As you continue reading, you are going to experience a miracle in your own life. I know because it happened to me. By using the powers of my subconscious and developing the reality of my Higher Self, my rheumatoid arthritis began to improve within six months. In my travels over the United States, I have seen miracles happen to many men and women who used the ideas in this book.

Ask yourself why certain people are sad and why others are happy. Why are some joyous while other people are absolutely miserable? Why are some prosperous when others are very poor? Why do some wonderful, kind, religious people suffer in mind and body while others who are not so kind or religious prosper? Continue reading and you will find the answers to these questions. The next chapter deals with love, which must become an integral part of your life if you are to finally take charge of your inner powers.

Before I close this chapter, I would like to remind you about a man who was not very successful by our standards. He never owned anything in his life. His entire professional career lasted only thirty-six months. He never traveled more than 150 miles from home. He never wrote a book. Most of us could not understand the language he spoke. Yet he had a greater impact on our existence than any force since. If you recall, He walked up and down the shores of Galilee. As He spoke, people listened. He said in one sentence what I have been trying to tell you in this chapter: "Be ye transformed by the renewing of your mind." In other words, if you change your thoughts, you can change your destiny.

Love is the one word that can evoke a response from the romantic and cynic alike. But which is the correct response? What do we really know of love? In *The Art of Loving*, Erich Fromm defines love as an attitude rather than a relationship to a specific person.* This attitude determines how a person relates to the world as a whole, not to just one particular person. Fromm says that a person who loves only one other person and is indifferent to all other people has mistaken love for enlarged egotism.

To this rather clinical definition we should add what Paul wrote about the attitudes of love in his first epistle to the Corinthians. Paul stated that love is always patient and kind, love is never jealous, love is never boastful or conceited, love is never rude or selfish, love does not take offense and is not resentful. Love does not take pleasure in other people's sins; it takes pleasure in light and truth. It is always ready to excuse, to trust, to hope, and to endure whatever comes.

This chapter about love begins with self-love because without self-love there is no love. When I was growing up, I was

*Erich Fromm, *The Art of Loving* (New York: Harper & Row Publishers, Inc., 1974).

er to love others than to love myself.
difficult to love myself, finding it much
Erich Fromm pointed out, this is not
before I can really love anyone else,

LOVE YOURSELF

I spent thirty-seven years in my body and not once did I ever tell my body that it was beautiful, lovely, perfect, whole, or that I loved it. Whenever I got out of the bathtub, I looked in the mirror and saw things that I wanted to change, thinking "this is ugly," "that is fat." Looking at my face in a mirror, I never saw the beauty; instead, I saw a nose that is not straight enough, eyes that should be a deeper blue, a mouth that should be fuller, ears that should be larger, and teeth that should be straighter.

Then a few years ago, I learned a technique that helped me do one of the most difficult things in my life—to love myself. A very wise man told me to look at my eyes in a mirror several times a day and say, "I love you" for thirty days. Well, that was impossible. At first I told him that I just could not do it. He answered that I must because I did not like myself.

I did some soul searching to see why I could not look at myself in the mirror. Thinking back to when I was about thirteen years old, I remembered baby-sitting for a lady who told me, "You have bedroom eyes and when you walk down the street you're always flirting." She probably did not realize how that hurt me; most likely, she was just trying to help my mother keep me in line. I could not imagine that I appeared to be flirtatious. I felt dirty; from that time on, when I was with other people, I would never look into anyone's eyes.

Even before that, I could remember that whenever my grandmother saw me looking in the mirror, she would say: "No, no, that's showing vanity, you know; your ego is showing." As a result of this negative programming from other people, I habitually avoided looking into anyone's eyes and looking at myself.

As soon as I understood why I was a thirty-seven-year-old woman who could not look at herself with love, I resolved to work on looking at myself in a mirror. At first, I would stick out my tongue and say, "Hi, Patricia, I love you," and stick my tongue out again, laughing about it. It took me a little longer than a month to master this technique.

After a month and a half, I awoke one morning with a great deal of love for the world. I remember jumping out of bed and running to the bathroom mirror. Spontaneously, I looked in the mirror and said, "Patricia, I really do love you," and smack, I kissed myself in the mirror. As I drew back from the mirror, my eyes locked with the reflection of my eyes in the mirror. I remember feeling such warmth and love; the eyes in the mirror looked back at me and said, "I love you, too." That is when I realized that I was not alone, that something greater than myself walked with me. This was the first time in my entire life that I experienced the presence of my Higher Self and knew that the Infinite Intelligence was there in me at that very moment. For the first time, I realized that I could fight for that person in the mirror. I could no longer let people walk all over me as I had in the past because something great, greater than me, was in there.

If you do not like yourself very much, use this technique. Look in the mirror and say, "I love you" to the image you see. Do this for thirty days and you will find that there is Someone with you, too.

PICTURES GUIDE THE MIND

Dr. Maxwell Maltz, a famous plastic surgeon, said that our minds work in words and pictures.* You have a mental picture, or a self-image, that governs your conduct and your outlook.

*Maxwell Maltz, *Psycho-Cybernetics* (New York: Simon and Schuster, Inc., 1968).

When you love yourself and feel proud of your self-image, you feel self-confident. Conversely, when you do not like yourself, your self-image is an object of shame, which you hide rather than express. The type of person you feel you are determines your way of life and the life you live. The human mind is like a computer that returns whatever picture it is fed. Remember that old data processing adage, "Garbage in, garbage out," and begin feeding your mind only positive pictures of yourself.

In his book, *Psycho-Cybernetics*, Dr. Maltz stated that he was amazed by the dramatic changes in his patients' characters and personalities resulting from the correction of physical defects through plastic surgery. He said that sometimes the operation created an entirely new person, transforming not only the patient's appearance, but also his or her whole life. In some cases, patients had talked themselves into plastic surgery because they blamed imaginary physical faults, such as large noses or protruding ears, for their unhappiness. Instead of operating on their noses or ears, Dr. Maltz operated on their self-images so that the patients could see themselves as they are and learn to love their images.

In *The Power of Positive Thinking*, Dr. Norman Vincent Peale tells a beautiful story about a Persian prince who was born with a hunchback.* This story illustrates the importance of self-image and the power of your subconscious. On his twelfth birthday, the prince's father offered his son any gift he wanted. To the proud king's surprise, the prince chose a statue of himself. The boy asked that the statue be carved with a perfect body, straight, and well-shaped. When the statue was finished, it was placed in the palace garden. At the beginning of each day and just before going to bed, the prince stood before the statue and said, "This is me. This is the way I shall grow up. This is my face, my body. This is the way I shall look to others." That dream became a picture and the picture became rooted in the prince's mind and heart. It was fused with desire and emotion. Each night he

*Norman Vincent Peale, *The Power of Positive Thinking* (New York: Fawcett Book Group, 1978).

stretched out straighter in his bed; each day he walked a bit more erectly. As he grew into manhood, he became exactly like the statue, straight and tall, perfect in body and stature.

The world is full of Persian princes who are living examples. You can be one, too.

If you think about this story for a moment, you will realize that the Persian prince used several of the techniques I mentioned in Chapter 1 to achieve his tall, straight body. He said affirmations about how his body would look, visualized how straight he would be, and prompted his subconscious with these positive thoughts each night before sleeping. To defeat rheumatoid arthritis ten years ago, I used the same techniques with prayer and meditation, as well as study of the subconscious mind and the Bible. After a friend gave me Dr. Peale's book, I read the story of the Persian prince. Because of this story, I believed I could straighten my own body in the same manner. And I did!

TREAT YOUR BODY LIKE THE TEMPLE IT IS

Is it any wonder that our bodies react the way they do when they are so often ignored? Talk love to your body; tell your body that it is beautiful. Send some kind thoughts inside, to the inner you, so that your body hears words of praise and blessing. Your body needs so much attention and love. It waits for your mental instructions. Tell your body how precious it is to you and how happy you are to be in it. Thank it for all the wonderful functions that it does. Say to yourself before you go to bed at night, "I am perfect, I am whole, I am loved, my body is loved." When you awaken and shower, look in that mirror and tell your body how wonderful it is. Talk to the cells that are so alive and hear everything you say. Realize that if you continue saying things like "My body will never be perfect nor whole" or "My body is always going to be fat," your body will act out your commands.

TAKE CHARGE OF YOUR LIFE

Dr. Elisabeth Kübler-Ross said that people who have not really lived scream the loudest on their death beds. In *On Death and Dying*, she says these people never took an active part in life; they just stood back and looked on.* They never took risks.

Each of us needs to take risks in order to live and love. Recall your childhood; children are notorious risk-takers. Remember when the world was a wondrous mystery, when you had to understand every nook and cranny, when you wanted to touch and feel everything. Experience life again.

Form the habit of taking charge of your thoughts. Be as certain as you were when you were a child that you have the right to happiness; stop condemning yourself. Do not become a martyr. The Supreme Intelligence does not intend you to do this. Learn to keep harmonious thoughts in your mind in order to succeed. Dwelling on past mistakes will just slow your progress. Claim that the Infinite Intelligence is with you and wants you to have what you are decreeing; claim it. Claim the power that is within your being through prayer.

Become a friend to yourself. When someone is your friend, you take that person as she is; it does not matter how she looks, she is your friend. You are not critical, you do not snub her, you accept her. Do not judge yourself any more than you would judge your friends. Look at yourself and accept yourself as a friend. If you feel inferior, not worthy of being your best friend, use an affirmation to reprogram your mind. Pray to your Higher Self for help.

When building a new house, you, the owner, would carefully consider each detail in the blueprints. Every feature—from doorknobs to bathroom closets—would be perfect; nothing less would do. Take charge of your mind like this; build it perfectly, and magical things will happen to you. Ask for what you want,

*Elisabeth Kübler-Ross, *On Death and Dying* (New York: Macmillan Publishing Co., Inc., 1969).

visualize it, believe that you will receive it and you will. Any picture you hold in your mind, supported by faith, will be given to you by your subconscious mind.

If you find that things are not manifesting in your life, then review your own thinking. Are you worrying about something from the past? Is there someone in your life that you have not forgiven? Are you feeling so guilty that you hate yourself, even though you appear self-righteous to others? Is there jealousy in your heart? Tear out whatever is poisoning your life. No matter what it is, remember that the Supreme Intelligence has decreed, "Old things are passed away; behold, all things become new." Step forward now and claim your happiness on this earth.

Do not be discouraged if things do not happen fast enough for you. Occasionally, only time can transform those thoughts that can change your destiny. It takes time to progress. Know in your heart that your life will change and that the wonderful things you desire will increase in your life. Continue to work steadily with your whole heart; as you search for the truth, it will be revealed to you. You will receive those gifts that your heart desires.

LOVE YOUR SPOUSE

George Leonard commented that although we can orbit the earth and touch the moon, this society has not devised a way for two people to live together for seven straight days with any assurance of harmony. Statistics prove his point; one in every two marriages in the United States ends in divorce. The average relationship lasts approximately six weeks. Frightening figures? Yes, but only if we do not learn all we can about love or if we do not take time to learn everything possible about the other person. Recently, I counseled a husband and wife who had been married for thirty-five years. The husband did not know his wife's favorite color nor did he know her dress size. He did not even know her middle name. The wife knew nothing about her husband's favorite sport, football. After thirty-five years, I should not have had to send them home with specific suggestions about how they could get to know one another, but I did.

Are you trying, struggling to save your marriage? Or has your marriage lapsed into a state of boredom, broken up only by bickering? The end of a marriage is not always a dramatic affair: There may be no unfaithfulness, no desertion, no blows—just the slow accumulation of dissatisfactions, a gradual growth of misunderstandings and irritations, until one person cannot stand it any longer. Tragically, many individuals do not sense what is happening to their marriages or have any idea how to stop it.

Any man or woman who wants to discover the building blocks of a happy and lasting marriage can do so. Begin by seeing your spouse as something more than a body to be clothed and fed; there is a soul in there, a soul that wants to be loved. Love is kindness, the same unselfish attention that came so naturally during your courtship. Love is believing in your companion. Love is thinking and expressing appreciation rather than criticism. The words "I'm proud of you" will do wonders for your lifelong companion. Why do we have kind words for others throughout the day but let down as soon as we cross our own threshold? Tell your family daily that you love them dearly and tell your spouse even more often. Great happiness is comprised of little kindnesses like these.

Be Spontaneous. Boredom and routine are two potholes on the road to your golden wedding anniversary. Spontaneity can smooth out that road and make the trip much more interesting. If you get up every morning, put the coffee on, eat the same brand of cereal, talk the same talk, read the same newspaper, go to work, come home, watch the same television programs, brush your teeth, and go to bed, I am talking directly to you. Granted, you and your spouse must do certain routine chores to keep your household going, but you can vary the routine. Buy your wife a beautiful flower, just one rose to brighten her day. Enclose a love

44

note when you bag your husband's baloney sandwich and he will think he is eating steak. If your wife has been doing all the cleaning, offer to vacuum. Make his favorite dinner, even though it's not his birthday. Do crazy things together. Honeymoon more often. If you look at your spouse and the old spark has been replaced with a ho-hum feeling and if you fantasize snuggling up to your electric blanket more often than your spouse at the end of the day, you have not necessarily fallen out of love—you are just getting bored.

When you do not have much money to spend, stretch your imagination instead. You do not have to go to a fancy restaurant or an expensive nightclub. First, convince one of your friends to take the children for the night. You can do the same for them next week. Make a date with your spouse. Then get a few candles, a bottle of cheap wine, and some hamburgers and french fries or a pizza. Romance each other. Listen to your favorite music on the radio. Most importantly, listen to each other and get back in touch with the person you could not stand being separated from before you were married.

I do not have to tell anyone who is married that loving someone does not automatically mean that you will agree about everything. When you disagree, fight fair by sticking to the topic. Do not rehash past arguments or unload those irrelevant salvos you have been saving up to prove your points. Try to listen to the other side (which just may make a lot of sense). Never go to sleep at night until disagreements with your marriage partner are settled. While you are asleep, unsolved problems become set in your mind as attitudes. Although there may be forgiveness and loving attention the next day, the scar remains. Say the words "I love you" in moments of tension and misunderstanding. Sometimes you will need to add three words that will be much harder to say: "I was wrong." There are times when a heart cannot be healed without those words.

Fears, angers, resentments, and bitterness not only lay the groundwork for divorce but actually poison the bodies of the persons involved. This includes those persons who overhear your

45

shouting matches. No one's body was made for hate. Your body, mind, and soul were created for happiness and good will. If these are missing in your marriage, use the affirmations in Chapter 9 to improve your marriage and love relationships.

DIVORCE

Psychiatrist David Viscott wrote a book, *The Language of Feelings,* in which he suggests moving out when a relationship becomes dull and sluggish.* Do not feel guilty, Viscott says, because lasting relationships between any two people in our generation are no longer practical. This means that when I am tired of you and you are tired of me, or if it seems like we have to work at our relationship, we can just split.

Viscott was so busy studying the effect that he overlooked the cause. Whether you are married or divorced, if you find yourself moving from one relationship to another, chances are that each time you will find yourself meeting the same person with a different face. The same circumstances happen all over again because you are running away from your problem. You will continue to meet this problem in a new guise at every turn in the road. I suggest that you meet that problem where you are, right now.

When you have sorted out all your reasons and thought about what went wrong, maybe it will not be too late. If you can learn from your mistakes, you will not have to keep repeating them. If you have not learned a lesson, you may need to stay where you are; you cannot progress because you will draw the same problem to yourself again. For example, so many women want to marry men with very strong personalities in order to have someone to lean on. If, however, these women are very independent, strong-willed, and aggressive, there could be a problem. When they choose someone so like themselves,

*David Viscott, *The Language of Feelings* (New York: Pocket Books, Inc., 1977).

46

possessing the same qualities, then there will be two bosses in the same house. Like two fires without enough wood, they will burn out. In Chapter 6, more will be discussed about recognizing lessons in the problem areas of our lives.

If you begin solving the problem in your marriage through prayer, you will find that spiritual truth will manifest. I have seen marriages saved, even though they were on the point of being dissolved, when one partner began praying. A new person evolved from that prayer, and the couple found happiness together. I suggest that if you are running from one marriage to another, or from one boyfriend or girlfriend to another, that you may be repeating old conditions and you may need to fight your problem right where you are with prayer.

In a few cases, prayer is not the whole answer. There is a limit to what a man or woman can be expected to endure in marriage. In these exceptional cases, a dissolution would probably be best for all concerned. Allow your Higher Self to make that decision for you. The Infinite Intelligence decides each case individually, according to the people involved and the reason that they married in the first place. This Supreme Intelligence is too wise to issue an edict banning divorce. If you are uncertain about divorcing your spouse and you do not know what to do, claim the divine wisdom of your Higher Self and pray. Ask for guidance about what you should do. After repeated prayer, you will find that either the conditions will change in your life or you will be given the way in which you can dissolve the marriage for the good of all concerned.

Recently, I heard a minister on television advise young people who were thinking about getting married to remember that marriage is for life, "till death do you part." Otherwise, he claimed, they would be condemned to hell. He went on to say that each of us has only one chance and that we should think about marriage thoroughly before we attempt it.

I wish I could have responded to that minister—to tell him that as a young person growing up, I thought about marriage. In my heart I believed that the man I married would be the only man for me for life. Young and blinded by inexperience, I was not wise enough to know that I was seeking a father in the husband I married. I tried to do everything right. I prayed every day and went to confession and took communion every week. I was an obedient, loving wife, yet my marriage fell apart; perhaps my expectations fell apart, also. As a young woman, I was told to live with loneliness, pain, heartache, and loss of respect. When I stopped accepting these expectations, the marriage was over.

We do not always die quickly; sometimes we die a little each day. If my husband and I had not divorced, I would have died. My body was slowly falling apart. I was experiencing stomach problems with aches and pains. Like so many married people today who are slowly dying, I refused to let go and let the Supreme Intelligence rule. Afraid to take a risk, many married people look to their spouses to fulfill all their needs. They live in a state of possession rather than in a state of love. If they only looked to the Supreme Intelligence, everything else would be given to them. The Higher Self I have come to know does not wish anyone to remain in a situation full of misery, hate, and resentment.

The Supreme Intelligence is not a part of some marriages because these marriages are based on mistaken ideas of love, infatuation, or love of a person's traits rather than love of the whole person. Young people have an awesome responsibility concerning marriage and love. They are asked to make a lifetime decision based on love, when love is something they may or may not have learned about. Examine your own childhood and see yourself as a flower that unfolds to the degree it is loved. Did praise and affection cause your flower to begin unfolding very early in life? If, on the other hand, you never experienced love as a child growing up, never knew what it meant to be caressed, you will love only to that degree. Your flower will open only in proportion to the love you received as a child. Each person reading this probably has areas that have not been unfolded through love. This does not mean that most parents are unfit, but even very loving parents can only give to their children to the degree in which love has been given to them.

Love and Be Loved: Overcome the Barriers. Sadly, there are many barriers to loving and being loved. While counseling families, I have found family members who have fears of being alone. Yet they do not know how to reach for someone else or whom they should reach. They are insecure within themselves; they have never been taught to love themselves and, although surrounded by family, they are afraid of being alone. So much of our present outlook is influenced by what happened to us as children: was negative input deeply imbedded into your mind as you grew up and were you called "stupid" or told, "You'll never make anything of your life."? The degree to which a person has a guilt complex and low self-esteem will govern how that person loves others because no one can love anyone else if he does not love himself. Complicating the matter is that persons with low self-esteem are sometimes difficult to love because they have a great deal of self-pity and despair.

The first person who asks a person with low self-esteem to marry may be an alcoholic or a jailbird, but these qualities will not be carefully considered: Because of low self-esteem and guilt, such a person will marry with relief, wondering how the other person could possibly love him. A person with low esteem attracts other people with low esteem. People with guilt feelings and low self-esteem need to release, let go, and let the Supreme Intelligence rule. The degree to which we love or hate ourselves as human beings is the degree to which we will be able to love somebody else.

Only through the silence of meditation did I learn how to expand my ability to love. By developing my mind's powers and studying *The Art of Loving* by Erich Fromm, books by Sigmund Freud, and the Bible, I become aware of the breadth and depth of love. Upon reflection, I have found that most of the loves in my life were conditional, filled with jealousy, hate, violence at times, competitiveness, and ambition; the relationships were based on infatuation. I loved one boy because he was cute or muscular. I loved another because of his curly hair or his big blue eyes.

I can well understand how many people thought that at one time they were in love when, in actuality, they were experiencing infatuation, physical attraction, or mutual curiosity. When it came down to being able to talk and have insights or establish stability in the relationship, these couples would look to the future to solve their problems. A rosy fog shrouded the imperfections that later aggravated the relationship.

How many women have thought and sometimes said, "Oh, he'll grow up; I'll change him when I marry him." They succeed in changing the men they marry: Their spouses stop smoking, drinking, and driving too fast. "I put him through school and got him where he is today. If it weren't for my working and my money," they claim, "he would not have those fancy clothes and that beautiful car." Meanwhile, these husbands are telling their friends, "If it weren't for her money, she wouldn't have me." And so the husband and wife live in a power struggle, not in love.

How many times have people said:

- I married her because she was frail and petite; now I am divorcing her because she is weak and helpless.

- I married him because he was so handsome; now all he thinks about is his looks.

- I married her because she was so intelligent and witty; now all she does is prove her points by constantly showing off her mind.

- I married him because he was rational and sensible and I knew that he would always have money; now I cannot stand being around him because he is such a bore.

- I married him because I knew he would be a good provider—I liked the way he made money; now all he thinks about is his business.

- We married each other because of sexual attraction; now we have nothing in common.

From these examples, you can appreciate how easy it is to marry for reasons other than love and realize that love is never a viable part of these relationships. If any of these describe your situation, ask your Higher Self for guidance and be willing to let go and allow the Supreme Intelligence to rule.

TOUCH THOSE YOU LOVE

Recently, a survey on touching took place in a university library. In each situation, the first man came in and handed a library card and book to a woman librarian without touching her. Then a second man came in and touched the librarian while handing her a book and library card. Each time the surveyors asked if there was any difference in the librarian's response to the two men, the librarian answered that she responded only to the man who touched her.

If you have been married for many years and have gotten out of the habit of touching your partner, do not assume that your spouse doesn't want to be caressed. You need to touch each other more often; make love to a person, not just to a body. Feel and touch and love each other as though you never touched, felt, or loved before. Remember, the marriage lasts only as long as the honeymoon lasts.

Fathers and mothers, kneel down and look in your children's eyes; talk to them. Grasp their hands or cup their faces in your hands and talk to them. Let them see you from where they stand, not from where you stand. It can be a bit frightening for a child to gaze up at a big giant. When you come down to their size, they will listen because you are near. Kneel down; talk to them, touch them.

LOVE OTHERS

Periodically, I ask my students, "If you were told that you had only twenty-four hours to live, what would you do?" Some of the students say, "Well, I'd call my mother and my dad and tell them I love them," or "I'd tell my children that I care and that I love them very much." Tell the people you love that you love them as if you had only twenty-four hours to live. Live life today as though there were no tomorrow and you will never be sorry when you leave this earth. You will have done everything you needed to do before you left, especially if you begin now.

Usually I skim the newspaper rapidly, but one day a particular headline caught my eye: "Love Gave Baby Life." The story was about a little girl who came into this world so diseased that the nurses handling her wore gloves to protect themselves from infection. No one, including the little girl's mother, wanted her. Born with congenital syphilis and rubella, porous bones, and a heart defect, she weighed less than twenty-four ounces. Doctors at the University of Illinois' high-risk nursery diagnosed the infant as blind and deaf. They said her condition would worsen, but they were wrong.

Six years later, this baby had grown into a lively, normal kindergarten graduate about to enter the first grade. Naturally, new medicines and technologies played a role in her amazing recovery. Doctors, however, credit one woman's love for an abandoned baby as the key to the child's recovery. That one woman was the licensed practical nurse who adopted the child as her special charge. At first, the nurse held her often; later, she wrapped her in a sling and carried her on her back as she cared for other babies in the hospital nursery. The doctors believed that the love the nurse provided helped to nurture the child back to health.

THE OLD AND THE YOUNG

Truly, love can make all the difference; sometimes, as in the previous story, it can mean the difference between life and death. Unfortunately, most of us use the power of love as little as we use the power of our subconscious minds. When I talk with senior citizen groups, I always ask if they are interested in meeting other people. "Oh, yes," a lady may reply, "but I'm afraid to say 'Hello.' " Then I ask if she responds to a stranger's greeting and she says, "Oh, I couldn't answer back. I'm too shy." How unfortunate that wonderful people like this woman are not able to reach out to other human beings, to bridge the gap between two people. Each time, I remind the senior citizens to avoid becoming imprisoned in themselves, and to instead reach out and make new friends. People need others with whom they can share secrets and inner selves, knowing that they will be accepted as they are without such comments as "I told you so."

As people grow older, they often forget that their "flower" is still unfolding; instead, they just stop growing. In many cases the elderly fulfill their own preconceived ideas about aging. When sixty-year-old people living full, active lives think that they will not be able to take care of themselves when they reach age seventy, they will probably *not* be able to take care of themselves in their seventh decade: Negative self-programming will fulfill this prediction. Statistics indicate that suicide occurrences increase consistently with age until age 80.

Ages of suicide victims	Percentage of U.S. population*
50 to 59 years	17.7 percent
60 to 69 years	18.3 percent
70 to 79 years	21.6 percent
80 years and older	20.2 percent

These sad statistics are a commentary not only on how older Americans view their lives but also on how we treat old people and how we feel about them. Imagine how massive doses of love could alter these statistics!

Older people have so much to give to young children—they should not be stashed away in nursing homes. Recent federal programs that combine senior citizens with children in day care have proved that young people help the old stay young and old people are eager to take time for the young. The extended family

*Source: Data from National Center for Health Statistics for 1978, Washington, D.C.

often provides a balance of ages and personalities. If you have elderly relatives, consider welcoming them into your family.

At the other end of our human continuum, adolescents are in the category of the highest rising suicide rates. At fifteen or sixteen years of age, and even as young as twelve, adolescents do not know what life is all about; and yet they end their lives before experiencing them. Our society needs to let these kids know how wonderful they are. We need to pat them on the back instead of criticizing them. Adolescents do not need to hear that they are stupid or that they will never become anything—no one does. They need our love and support. Self-esteem develops as a child gets older; it is fed by the child's parents and the child's environment. Even if you are not a parent, you *are* part of the environment. Do not treat the adolescents in your neighborhood as if they were lower than you; treat them with respect and they will earn it.

Burgeoning alcohol and drug problems reveal that many kids today do not like themselves. Remember how it felt when you were growing up and you had pimples on your face—how ugly you felt? Telling a child to ignore his condition and sending him back into the world to grin and bear it isn't enough. You can't expect him to simply adjust; you have got to help him. Teach the child to feel good inside, and the outside will improve; you can help your child to overcome his insecurities. It will take a lot of time, talk, and love to ensure that your child's self-esteem is high.

While lecturing in New York City, the Dahli Lama said that our greatest duty, our main duty, is to help others. Then he smiled and added, "And please, if you can't help them, would you please not hurt them?" Helping and loving our friends and relatives is usually not difficult; liking a complete stranger is different. You may not like his actions, looks, or idiosyncracies. Whenever you take an instant dislike to someone, try to look beyond that person's physical appearance or irritating traits. Look straight through to the Higher Self in that person; you will find something that you can like because that same Infinite Intelligence in that person is in you. Be patient; it takes time to love the Infinite Intelligence within someone. The nicest thing happens when you realize that you do not have to feel guilty about not liking the physical person, certain actions, or traits; you have only to love the Infinite Intelligence within.

Because thoughts really exist, they go out into the universe where they manifest, take control of your thoughts. Carefully select the thoughts that occupy your mind. Do not entertain thoughts of hate for your neighbor: thoughts of wanting to steal, or thoughts of adultery, lust, or vengeance. If you harbor these feelings, inner thoughts will eventually materialize. Sound out goodness to people who try to hurt you; understand that somewhere deep inside them they have an awful lot of pain that causes them to try to hurt you. Pray to the Higher Self within each of them and you will see things begin to change. If you return love for love, you will receive love; but if you return hate for hate, you will also receive hate. The first thing you need to do is release resentment and hostility (this is explained in Chapter 6). Then create a state of mind filled with peace and harmony and send this positive good out to those who hurt you. When you do, you will notice that the situation will right itself.

THE WHITE-CROSS TECHNIQUE

If you have a boss who always makes life difficult for you or if you have constant problems with a co-worker, try the white-cross technique. Visualize a white cross over that person's head and start sending loving thoughts to the Higher Self within that person. Mentally say, "You do not wish to harm me. You are becoming more loving; you are a much more loving person." When you say this and see the white cross in your mind's eye, you will notice a different expression on that person's face. If the person has been nasty, he will become suddenly quiet; if he has been angry, he will start to speak more softly. The white cross protects you; with it no one can harm you. Something inside the other person yearns to be soft, kind, and loving in the presence of the white cross. Therefore, when you concentrate on the divine presence within those people who wish to harm you, their expressions will be altered.

You can use this technique whenever you are in the company of people who are talking negatively, or gossiping, about other people. All you have to do is mentally place the white cross over the gossips' heads and they will begin to change within their own consciousnesses. This is especially helpful when you do not want to be part of such a discussion but are unable to leave.

RECEIVING FROM OTHERS

Is it more blessed to give than to receive? Not always. Throughout my life, I have had difficulty in receiving. I love to give, but when others try to give to me, I just cannot receive gracefully. To demonstrate how stubborn I can be, when I first began giving classes to share what I had learned about the subconscious, I started with four women at my kitchen table. Then one day no one showed up for class. This seemed odd to me because they had all seemed to be enjoying my classes. So I called one of the women and asked why none of them had showed up. She answered that the group felt in taking my time and information, they should give me something in return. Previously when this topic had been discussed, I had absolutely refused to accept any donations. But now, after settling on a suitable donation, all four returned to class and I have been teaching classes ever since. Fortunately no longer in the kitchen.

One would think that I had learned my lesson, but I didn't. And as I said before, when a lesson is not learned, the problem continues to return. Something inside of me kept saying that I could do it myself and no one should have to do anything for me. Then one day a very dear friend of mine reminded me that once again I was stopping anyone who tried to give to me from receiving the joy and blessings of giving. And this time I learned my lesson.

Even if you do not experience joy in receiving, remember that as you give, you receive. Do not stop another person from receiving by not letting them give to you. Allow those who have been wanting to help you, and are willing to give to you, to do so. Remember, only a martyr wants to do everything and give everything, and receive nothing. The Supreme Intelligence does not want *anyone* to be a martyr.

In this chapter, I have shared with you what I have discovered about love: That it is essential to love yourself before you can love anyone else, that infatuation and physical attraction sometimes masquerade as love, and that prayer and love can work miracles. In the next chapter, I will discuss discovering your hidden potential and setting goals. You must love yourself before you can put these concepts into practice.

FIVE

Your Hidden Potential

Your first duty to yourself is to develop your own unique personality so that you can take your proper place in life. This is not as easy as it sounds because we tend to become brainwashed about the greatness of others—frequent media coverage and efficient press agents keep us informed about the rich and famous. Self-development has been replaced by hero worship for the famous. One hero worshipper tried to murder the President of the United States to gain the attention of the actress he worshipped. Of course, this is an extreme case; most of us are satisfied with an E.T. sweatshirt, Arnold Palmer golf clubs, a Michael Jackson album, a Gloria Vanderbilt blouse, a Pittsburgh Steelers jacket, or a Mr. T haircut.

As they grow up, children try to emulate movie stars, athletes, and other famous people. By looking to others, they overlook the opportunity to look inside themselves to see their own hidden potential. Wrapped up in adulation, they need to be coached by parents or counselors to be more introspective. If adolescents continue to pattern themselves after their heroes, they will try to duplicate the acceptance their heroes receive.

rs later, they will live out their adult lives vicariously, forgetting the most important and unique individuals in their lives—themselves.

Take the responsibility for becoming the very best person that you can become—a unique person with personal goals, not a duplicate of someone else. Accept the role that was given to you at birth: to become a great person in your own right. When you look below your surface self to meet the true you, you will be able to give the world a unique contribution—yourself. Look deep inside while setting your goals, and your hidden potential will come forward.

SET GOALS FOR YOURSELF

Do you drift along day after day, not knowing where you are going or having any idea of how to improve your life? This type of behavior is contrary to human nature. As Aristotle said, "Man is a goal-seeking animal and his life has meaning only if he is reaching out and striving for his goal." So you see that one way to improve your life is to establish definite goals for yourself; otherwise, you become a victim of circumstance. When you do not have goals in your life, you are more influenced by what other people think than by what *you* think or feel. When you do not set goals, you are at the mercy of somebody else when you buy clothing, a car, or even when you take a vacation.

Do you find yourself turning to someone else for advice rather than making a decision on your own? If so, chances are that as you were growing up, you were programmed to think that someone else's opinion was necessary because you could certainly not decide for yourself. Unfortunately, your desires will never be satisfied until you begin setting goals for yourself; otherwise, you will be too busy satisfying other people's desires.

If you do not know what goals you should have, affirm, "My subconscious mind knows at all times what particular goals I need to be setting; my subconscious mind is providing me with this information at this very moment." Say this over and over again; eventually, you will form very definite ideas about what your purpose is or what goals you should be setting.

Have faith in your own goals and desires. Do not listen to people who say that you will never achieve your goals. Realize that you have the power within you to do anything that you want on this earth as long as you work toward your goal, practice it, and study it. Only negative programming can limit your achievement. Each of us uses such a small percentage of the Infinite Intelligence's most wonderful gift to us—our minds— that we have an unlimited potential. The difficulty is understanding how enormous that gift is.

See the Goal and Success Planner on pages 63–64. By using this planner, you can define your goals for every facet of your life. In order to have balance in your life, you must set goals for each part of your life so that you develop as a whole person. The last part of the planner, the Goal Affirmations and Images sheet, sums up your goals. Read this part at least once a day. Concentrate on each affirmation—visualize it. Decree it and thank your Higher Self for it.

There is something magical about writing down your goals, even the very simple things such as buying a new dress or suit, paying a dentist's bill, or providing for your child's schooling. If you are a newlywed, your list could include when you would like to have your first child, buy your first home, or begin investing in real estate or stocks.

By reading your list each evening and saying affirmations every night before going to bed, you will place these thoughts in your subconscious and your desires will manifest. It's a miracle! The first time I wrote down my goals, I was shocked when, within just a few days, these goals started to materialize in my life. As your goals begin to manifest, be sure to select higher goals to replace those that you have achieved.

Keep your Goal Affirmations and Images sheet as a private part of your life. Remember the Bible story about Jesus's healing a leper and then cautioning him not to tell anyone he was healed.

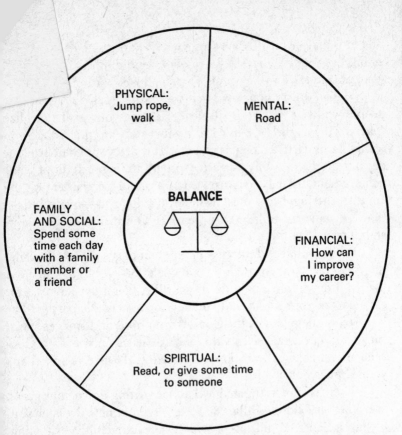

Figure 1. If you do not have all five areas of your life working for you, your life wheel will bounce and shimmy like a flat tire because your life is not in balance.

If the man had gone home loudly proclaiming that he was healed, some doubters might have told him that it would not last. His subconscious would have reacted to this, and his leprosy would have returned.

The same thing happens when you are setting goals. Do not give someone's negative thoughts a chance to become part of your goal setting. Hide your Goal Affirmations and Images list. Sometimes placing your list of goals in your Bible allows these goals to manifest in your life sooner. A few years ago, I started working with pyramid power: I place my affirmations under a cardboard pyramid, knowing that the energy in the pyramid is releasing my affirmations out into the universe. (If you would like to know more about pyramid power, write for information and my audiotape cassette. My address is on page 140.

GOAL AND SUCCESS PLANNER

In order to develop a positive self-image and to fulfill your purposes in life, you must set goals for each part of your life. Because goals are interrelated, you cannot separate family goals from work goals any more than you can separate physical goals from mental goals. By making goals and plans for each of the following areas on a sheet of paper, you will be developing yourself as a whole person—a person who will live a life filled with purpose and meaning. Remember to express your ambitions, dreams, and hopes—let your mind soar!

Career goals
- My long-range career goals (five years from now)
- My career will express my purpose in life in this way
- My plan for achieving my career goals
- My short-range career goals (one year from now)
- Specific actions I take each working day to achieve my career goals

Financial goals
- I will retire at the age of
- When I retire, my financial worth will be
- My long-range financial goals (five years from now)
- My plan for achieving my financial goals
- My short-range financial goals (one year from now)

- Specific actions I will take each day to achieve my financial goals
- My financial status will support my purpose in life in this way

Spiritual goals
- My long-range spiritual goals (five years from now)
- My spiritual goals will express my purpose in life in this way
- My short-range spiritual goals (one year from now)
- Specific actions I will take every day to achieve my spiritual goals

Physical goals
- My long-range physical goals (five years from now)
- My short-range physical goals (one year from now)
- Specific actions I will take every day to achieve my physical goals

Mental goals
- My long-range mental goals (five years from now)
- To achieve my career, financial, and spiritual goals, I must develop myself mentally in these ways
- Specific actions I will take every day to achieve my mental goals

Family and social goals
- My long-range family and social goals (five years from now)
- My purpose in life will find expression through my family and social goals in this way
- Specific actions I must take to achieve these long-range family and social goals

GOAL AFFIRMATIONS AND IMAGES

In order to achieve your goals, constantly reinforce them by saying affirmations and visualizing a related aspect of your self-image. To strengthen your inner resources and your determination to achieve your goals, write down at least one affirmation and one characteristic of the self-image for which you are striving.

Career goals
- My affirmation
- My self-image

Financial goals
- My affirmation
- My self-image

Spiritual goals
- My affirmation
- My self-image

Physical goals
- My affirmation
- My self-image

Mental goals
- My affirmation
- My self-image

Family and social goals
- My affirmation
- My self-image

Each of us has a marvelous potential in some way, a capacity to be activated. If you do not know what your true potential is, or if you doubt that you have any potential at all, start to look deep within yourself. Say an affirmation daily and you will find your potential. You may want to use an affirmation such as, "I ask my Higher Self to surface at this moment and show me my true potential in this lifetime." Each of us has a great yearning within ourselves to become more than we are, to tap the many wonderful things within each of us.

*Three steps to success**

1. Discover what you love to do, and then do it. If you do not know what you want, ask your subconscious mind for guidance. Say, "My Higher Self reveals to me my true place in life." Continue saying these words and it will come to you.

2. Specialize in some particular branch of work and find out more about it than anyone else; whether it is sweeping office buildings or brain surgery, be the best. Find the fastest or cleanest way to perform the task, and you will prosper.

3. Be sure that what you want does not lead to your success only. Your desire must not be selfish; it must benefit humanity.

One of the most exciting things in life is finding out more about yourself. Since only 3 to 10 percent of your brain power is regularly used, there is a lot left to delight and surprise you. Look for other skills and resources that you know you have. Make a list of specific things that you have always wanted to do; then make a list of your abilities and match these up with the things you have always wanted to do.

FULFILLING YOUR POTENTIAL

Frequently, magazines feature articles about people who did not realize they had certain abilities until they tried certain things. The examples are endless:

- Women who became successful entrepreneurs after, or while, raising families
- Men who left successful business careers to become ministers or priests

*Adapted from *The Power of Your Subconscious Mind*, by Joseph Murphy (Englewood Cliffs N.J.: Prentice-Hall, Inc., 1963).

- Professional athletes who left organized sports in order to write music

- Grandmothers who became VISTA volunteers

- Nuns who left their convents to enter politics

- Accountants who worked with troubled adolescents as an avocation

- Computer programmers who taught reading and basic skills to Asian immigrants

- Senior citizens who retired to become full-time volunteers in fields unrelated to their former careers

Each of us has the potential to do many things—probably more than we can cram into a lifetime. Do not be afraid to uncover all the facets of your potential. Be sure to keep a positive attitude; do not give up before you start by deciding that you are going to fail. Don't compromise by deciding that your life is pretty comfortable the way it is, so you really do not need to take chances by risking your security and peace of mind for something untried or unknown. People who do not take risks are dead; they may be physically breathing, but they don't *experience* life.

Sometimes the desire that you have within yourself is all you need to start fulfilling a particular desire. If you have a desire to write, sit down and write every day at the same time for fifteen minutes. Write down whatever thoughts come to mind, and allow the thoughts to flow. Eventually, if you do this day after day, you will create beautiful work. Later, you may want to take creative writing classes.

If you have had a desire to paint but you are not taking action, get some paint brushes and some books about painting, or take painting classes. You will be amazed at the marvelous things you can create. If you think you would enjoy singing, dancing, or playing a musical instrument, go to it. If you enjoy working with your hands, try carpentry, sewing, crocheting, wood carving, and so on. A work of art can unfold from your hands.

If you have been so busy sending your children to college but have not attended school yourself, find a class you are interested in and sign up. If you have always wanted to be more active in the community, begin by attending your city or town council meetings. If you have always wanted to start your own business, begin investigating today.

Age is never a problem when you desire to add a new dimension to your life. Grandma Moses became a famous artist at an advanced age. Cesar Franck composed his first symphony at age sixty-seven. Bernarr McFadden traveled to Europe at the age of eighty-four and proved that he was not getting old by parachuting into the sea. (Yes, he lived to tell about it.) George Bernard Shaw was still writing plays after he was ninety years old. Eighty-seven-year-old Helen Hooven Santmyer sold her epic novel, . . . *And Ladies of the Club*, which became a best-seller. What secret did all of these men and women share? They possessed a zest for life and enthusiasm. They were not afraid to develop their potential.

HILDEGARDE

Years ago, the headline read: "Men Hildegarde's Age Too Old to Date, She Says." The article described this then seventy-four-year-old singer as one who thinks young and practices absolute discipline to keep her figure trim. Hildegarde does not suffer from high blood pressure, obesity, or anything connected to tension.

"Don't use the word *elderly* to describe me," she chided softly. "I'm in that bracket, I know that, but I won't accept it. I just won't allow myself to slump. The spirit starts the brain. A person can be anything he or she wants. It's the power of the mind over matter. I think young." she said.

Hildegarde talks with extreme self-confidence. Her self-esteem is high and has buoyed her across the waters of fifty years of show business. This is the spirit in which Hildegarde has approached her life. She has controlled her life and, in the process, seems to have achieved a certain power over it.

YOUR UNLIMITED IMAGINATION

Imagination is the great power that shaped the destiny of our world and your individual destiny even before you picked up this book. A creative imagination helps you actualize your potential as a human being; it enables you to be successful in your job and everyday life. You will find that using your imagination makes you more open to new ideas and creative ways of doing things. You will not be stuck in the routine acts of daily life. The creative, imaginative you will be dissatisfied with the way things are going; you will create new ways, new courses, and new approaches to different problems.

Even though some imaginative people such as Shakespeare, Bach, and Dickens seemed to thrive under a great deal of pressure, most creative geniuses produced their greatest works in a relaxed state by using the power of their subconscious minds. Thomas A. Edison, for example, took catnaps throughout the day and came up with so many inventions that he was called the wizard of Menlo Park. Composer Wolfgang Mozart played billiards for relaxation; during this time, tunes popped into his head. Inventer James Watt discovered the secret of steam power while idly watching a kettle boil. Sir Isaac Newton was wandering around in his garden one day, watched an apple fall, and developed the theory of gravity. Marie Curie discovered radium while performing another experiment. Every day we read of people who use imagination to arrive at solutions to what had been unsolvable problems. With evidence such as this, who can doubt the power of the subconscious?

Use your self-knowledge, self-discipline, and the creative power of imagination to explore your hidden potential and master your fate. Imagination should not be confused with make-believe; that is, the single dimension of appearance. Imagination requires that once you arrive at a conclusion, you accept as true whatever you have imagined to be true. It is very important that you believe in your own powers; you cannot simply imagine what you believe. For example, you may use your imagination to visualize a great deal of money, enough to pay your bills and then some. Simultaneously, you may fear that so much money will ruin you or that your loved one will want you only for your money. This is make-believe; you have no faith in what you visualize.

Cultivate your imagination so that when you are affirming things, you can actually feel and see them. The ability to visualize and give instructions to yourself is known as *autosuggestion*, or self-hypnosis. Autosuggestion can control your whole personality; it can work for you but it can also work against you. If you see yourself overcoming obstacles and winning, you will win. If, however, you imagine yourself defeated, you will experience defeat. When the will and the imagination are at variance, the imagination always wins. If you find that affirmation and visualization are not working for you, review your mental images and root out the negative pictures; then your desires will manifest in your life.

MY FLIGHT FROM MY POTENTIAL

I believe that everyone on this earth was born with a special mission; when we were young, deep down inside of us there was a calling. Some of us accept this gift from the Supreme Intelligence and some of us do not. This calling can be to the ministry, to become a doctor, a parent, a bricklayer, a gardener, a writer, a poet, a singer, or an artist. Some of us pretend that we never heard the call. I pretended not to hear the call but my Higher Self kept calling.

My story begins in my grandmother's house on a beautiful mountain in West Virginia. We lived in a town so small that the sign said "Welcome to Hurricane," on one side and "You are leaving Hurricane" on the reverse. After my father walked out on the family, my sisters and I stayed with my grandmother while my mother found work and established a home for us in Cincinnati, Ohio.

Looking back, I can see that the struggle of my youth was the very beginning of my mission. The reason for my being where I am today began when that little lonely heart called out to God from the top of a mountain in West Virginia to ask Him to be with her. God knew that the real desire of that lonely heart was the deepest cry of the soul asking that His spirit never leave. That is the prayer He heard.

During the unfolding of my adolescence, the first faint suggestions that my Higher Self might some day call me to help others gnawed away at my restless awakening mind. When I first thought of the idea, it surprised me. As I grew older, I rejected the call from my Higher Self. I traveled from church to church to find answers that would help me fulfill the great bidding within. At the same time, I was determined to stifle those feelings that said, "You will serve."

I ran away from the call of my Higher Self and made my own plans. In those years, I was led deeper and deeper into perplexities that I had not counted on in my carefully calculated road to success. I tried to make my own rules; they failed. Unwilling to admit to anyone—much less myself—that I was confused, I continued to have a recurring suspicion that the thing I really wanted was the very thing I was fighting.

Over the years, I married and had children. God did not leave me alone; He allowed me to continue with what I desired. Like any father who truly loves his child, He stood back, watching and waiting. I continued walking in my own light, not His. My life became filled with more confusion and contradiction. I experienced only spurts of happiness during the years that I reared three children and went through a divorce. As I moved through the worlds of business and pleasure, mingling and talking with those I thought I admired, I rarely saw a truly happy face.

The pain of arthritis followed this period of emptiness. No matter what cures I sought, the pain remained. Little did I dream that during this terrible illness, I was standing on the threshold of a transforming experience that would bring my childhood dreams to fruition.

MY DREAMS BECOME REALITY

I learned a secret from Dr. Murphy's book, *The Power of Your Subconscious Mind*,* that would not only save my own restless soul but would help millions who are longing for that inner peace. While reading this book, I began to realize that I had been living in an outer world and would have to pay more attention to my inner world to be able to change the illness and pain in my life. (In Chapter 1, I described my recovery and the beginning of my mission.)

As I regained my health, I began to feel that little spark I had felt as a small child: that God had something planned for me and that He had planted something very deep in me that I had not permitted to grow. The words Paul wrote in his second epistle to the Corinthians now made sense: "Therefore, if any man be in Christ, he is a new creation. Old things are passed away. Behold all things are made new." The words of the Bible became messengers to my soul as I began to know the truth within me and the universe.

The truth is revealed when the soul finally surrenders itself in faith to the Higher Self. Then the power that no human eye can see creates a new being in the image of the Supreme Intelligence. No one sees the Supreme Intelligence, but the miracle is there. Today I know that this pen in my hand is commissioned to share truth with others, to share a power that will allow them to be free.

*Joseph Murphy, *The Power of Your Subconscious Mind* (Englewood Cliffs, N.J.: Prentice-Hall, Inc., 1963).

When you hear that small voice and decide to act on that call, how can you be certain that your decision will be in accord with the will of your Higher Self? If your decision is filled with love and goodness, it is the will of the Supreme Intelligence. If your decision is selfish or if it will harm another person, it is not the will of the Supreme Intelligence. Sometimes you will be called to do work that seems impossible; then you can be *positive* that it is the Supreme Intelligence's will because you cannot do it alone. At this point, to borrow Dr. Robert Schuller's phrase, impossibility thinking becomes possibility thinking.

A very dear friend of mine said that while he was growing up, he had wanted to be a doctor. He went to the university and majored in business administration. Then he thought again about becoming a doctor, but decided that the schooling would take too long. He then had a call to the ministry and became a minister. Today he is in the healing ministry. Now he is a doctor of the mind, spirit, and soul—perhaps a greater doctor than if he had become a medical doctor.

After reading this chapter, please set some goals for your life and adopt as one of your goals finding and fulfilling your potential. Do not let worries about finances, age, or failure stop you from fully expressing your potential. If it is something that you really want and can do, your Higher Self will show you the way. You will feel much more whole and in tune with your life and your Higher Self when you fulfill your potential.

The next chapter discusses how to release all of the frustrations, memories, hurts, and sorrows of life—how to let go and let the Supreme Intelligence rule. All of this weight from the past can destroy your peace of mind and slow down your pursuit of your potential.

SIX

Let Go and Let the Supreme Intelligence Rule

Job, that blameless and upright man in the Old Testament, probably never heard of the subconscious mind. Yet he posed a question that highlights the power of negative imagery when he asked, "Who can bring a clean thing out of an unclean?" With inspired, penetrating insight, he answered "Not one." Deep in our subconscious minds are negative inclinations and habits, fears, and insecurities that float like scum on the surface. Unless you release all of the negative images in your life that have strangled your power to live up to your full potential, you will continue to be unclean, confused, and frustrated. Toward the end of this chapter, I offer releasing techniques that can be used to clean the negative corners of your mind.

RELEASE NEGATIVE PROGRAMMING

William James, a psychologist in the mid-nineteenth century, said that the greatest discovery of his generation was that men could alter their lives by altering their attitudes. Think about it and you will realize that you are in charge of your own destiny—

you and no one else. Is your destiny in good hands? Go back for a moment and review your own life. Could it be that you have not been successful because you have not been very positive about your life? Of course, there are other people to blame: "It's because of my parents, the way they brought me up." "It's the way my teachers treated me." "My husband didn't appreciate me." or "My wife didn't love me enough."

I remember doing this, placing blame on someone else for where I was in life. Today, when I hear a woman whom I am counseling say, "It's my husband's fault that I'm sick," I bring her to the point of accepting the full responsibility for her illness; it is her mind that is causing her to be sick. She must reach a point where she can recognize the real problem.

Years ago, Walt Kelley's cartoon character Pogo summed up our situation in life when he said, "We has met the enemy and it is us." Once you realize that you can be your own worst enemy, then your life will start to change. Look at yourself!

- Are you a negative person?
- Are you always certain that things are going to go wrong?
- Are you suspicious of other people's good intentions?
- Do you criticize more than you compliment?
- Are you rude and inconsiderate to most people?

If you recognize these negative traits in yourself, do something about your negative attitude. (Notice that I did not say you should blame yourself; this would be wasted energy. Just resolve to do something about your negativity.)

Since infancy, most of us have been given negative suggestions that our subconscious minds have accepted:

- You can't.
- You must not.
- You'll fail.

- You're wrong.
- It's no use.
- You haven't got a chance.
- You'll never amount to anything.
- It's not what you know, it's who you know.
- The world is going to the dogs.
- What's the use, nobody cares.
- You're too old now.
- Things are getting worse.
- Love is for the birds.
- You can't trust a soul.
- You just can't win.
- It's not the right thing to do.

How many of those statements ring a bell with you? From this very moment, do not give life to these words. Disown them. When you find yourself trapped in a negative environment created by other persons' pessimism and suspicion, consciously affirm, "I can do all things through the power of my subconscious mind." Or use one of the other affirmations in Chapter 9 to flood your mind with positive thoughts.

RELEASE NEGATIVE ATTITUDES

Once you have released these negative statements from your life, do not add new attitudes. Your Higher Self does not require that you possess perfection of character. (Imagine how difficult it would be to live in this imperfect world if your Higher Self demanded perfection!) Your Higher Self does require that you *strive* for perfection. In order to strive for perfection, do not dwell upon negative thoughts such as, "I know I'm going to be sick," allowing this thought to burrow inside of your mind. Within seventy-two hours, this negative thought will become a reality in your body.

The next time you feel chilled or begin sneezing, do not escalate negative thought patterns by thinking, "I bet this cold will end up giving me bronchitis," or, "I'll probably get pneumonia." This type of thinking is merely a habit from the past. The first thing to do when you feel a chill or begin sneezing is to control your mind and refuse to accept the idea that you are going to be sick. Drive the thought away from your consciousness at that very moment by calling upon your Higher Self. Decree that through your higher Self, all things are possible and you have no need for this sickness.

Have you ever awakened feeling sick but told yourself that you must work and could not afford to be sick, and noticed later in the day that you felt much better? On another morning, when your work was not so pressing, you might awaken and give in to sickness. How many times have you heard someone complain about what was going to happen to him (such as catching the flu or taking a new medicine that will not work)? The chances are that he will catch the flu and the medicine will not work. If you were having your broken arm set in a doctor's office and thought, "It's going to take forever for this arm to heal," it would take longer than normal for the arm to mend. Seventy-two hours from the time that you say something, it will manifest in your life. Do not name your aches and symptoms because you give them credence in your subconscious mind by naming them. Your subconscious mind is eager to give you what you ask for.

Years ago, my son slashed his leg open while he was riding a dirt bike. Naturally, I wanted to reinforce his subconscious mind with healing thoughts but he would have none of it, so we went to the doctor's office. In the waiting room, Steve kept saying things like, "This will be worse than you think, Mom. I'll probably be in the hospital and they'll have to operate on my leg." I answered, "Steve, don't say that; there is nothing to be worried about," while fervently wishing that my son had not inherited

my stubborness. Two days after his leg was stitched
tor's office, the leg became so infected that we took
hospital, just as he had predicted. His negative att
fested in only seventy-two hours.

If you want your subconscious to attract money, avoid making negative statements such as, "I'm a little short this month,"
"I'll never be able to pay all these bills," or "My car's going to
be repossessed if I don't make a payment on it quickly." Being
a little short of money is like being a little sick; your subconscious
will see to it that these conditions worsen because it must fulfill
the situations you describe to it. Quite logically, condemning
those who are wealthier than you will convince your subconscious
that you most certainly do not want to be as wealthy as they
are. Similarly, if you regard money as evil or dirty, your subconscious will, too. (Because you cannot attract what you criticize, you will not have to worry about any filthy money coming
your way.) If you are in the habit of saying or thinking, "I can't
afford it," even though it may sometimes be true, break the habit.
Say instead, "I'll buy it; I accept it in my mind," with all the
conviction you can muster, and later it will be yours.

If you do not like your job, change those thoughts of "I
hate my work" to "My job is perfect for me and I am perfect
for my job." You should affirm these words every day—as often
as you are currently telling yourself that your job is terrible.
Eventually, by saying this affirmation, you will start to find that
perfect job, or things will change at work in such a way that
your job *will* be perfect for you. You might also affirm, "I can
do all things through the power of my subconscious mind."
Whatever you do, have no time for thoughts such as "I hope
they fire me."

By now you realize that if you expect poverty, you will
attract it. If you fear cancer, you will attract it. If you expect
failure, you will experience failure. Remember that your subconscious mind does not judge what is right for you; it simply
obeys orders and tries to please you.

You do not have to think about ulcers to have ulcers, but you can think ulcerous thoughts such as worry, resentment, hate, and hostility. Your body will follow your mental vision. Remember, you go where your vision is. If you want good fortune, think about good fortune and it will be yours. If you say, "I'm a jinx" or "A jinx is always following me," your subconscious will follow your orders and bring about all kinds of trouble in your life. If you break a leg and proclaim, "This is just the beginning; everything happens in threes," sure enough, a second problem will come, and then a third catastrophe will follow. Once you set up this pattern, your subconscious mind acts to make your statement come true.

When you feel that you are not able to cope with the trials of life and one disappointment follows another, you need to adopt a new, positive attitude that will produce immediate results. Remember that through your Higher Self, you have been given mastery over your own destiny. Do not decide that life is rejecting you; realize that you are rejecting yourself. If you are not receiving the things that you want, the reason is not because you are not entitled to have them. Your Higher Self wants you to have everything that you claim with conviction. Recognize that people do not have power over you, but that you have power over them. Your success and happiness will depend primarily on that hidden potential within you because this will give you greater self-esteem. When you start to notice accomplishments happening each day, you will insist on success and be moved in a direction where success will be part of your life.

Release and let go of the old concepts that miracles do not exist, that you are not worthy, and that you do not have the right to be a child of God and do the works of the Father. Remember that the Infinite Intelligence gave us dominion over His kingdom and ourselves. Once you claim this dominion, then your Higher Self will become a power in you. When a house has been wired for electricity, it lights up to the same degree as its source of energy. So, too, you are illuminated when you claim your connection to your Higher Self. Eliminate the negative doubts ingrained in you. Know that you have a right to the power within you; once you learn to develop this power, you will have a new kind of consciousness. This consciousness will set your world free; rather than being enslaved, you will be free to love, heal, and experience good.

Do not allow your mind to hold grievances of the past. Do not dwell on how terrible it was that you were born into a family that did not love you, or how someone may have hurt you at one point in your life. William Shakespeare said in *Hamlet*: "There is nothing either good or bad, but thinking makes it so." Use the releasing techniques in this chapter to release from your consciousness those negative memories from the past; do not hold these to yourself. The thoughts that you entertain today will be what is written for you tomorrow.

While you are learning to take charge of your thoughts, resist those negative thoughts that are caused by changes occurring in your daily life. You may receive news of an unfortunate happening in your life; for example, the death of your favorite aunt. If you dwell on that unfortunate happening, you can easily start to wallow in self-pity. Then your subconscious will be tied to that sorrowful condition; therefore, do not allow your mind to take hold of that condition. Change your attitude toward your aunt's death from sorrow for your loss to joy in her resurrection so that you may be spiritually benefited by your actions.

RELEASE THE OLD
TO MAKE ROOM FOR THE NEW

A woman who became famous by winning contests travels throughout the United States to speak to various groups, telling how she wins the contests and describing the houses she wins. This is how she does it: After entering a contest, she goes out and buys a lot. Next, she begins believing that the house in the contest is going to be on that lot. Then she wins the house! One of the secrets of her success is that she makes room for the new.

In my own life, I have found that whenever I wanted something badly, I would receive it after I surrendered similar objects that I did not really need, thus creating a place for the new. For example, if you have a closet of old clothes that you would like to replace with new clothes, create a space for the new. Give away your old possessions and you will be surprised with something new to replace what you have given away. Learn to make room for what you want. Look around your home, select objects that you are tired of, and slowly give some of them away; release them.

RELEASE THOSE YOU LOVE

Perhaps one of the most bitter lessons that I had to learn as a mother was to release my children. I wanted to instill so much knowledge in them, I had so many correct answers; then I began to notice that they also had the correct answers. They repeated to me what I had said to my mother: "I want to do it myself; I want to be on my own." Although wanting to teach my loved ones, I recalled the lessons I had learned and released them so that they would be able to experience what they needed to experience. It was not easy to let go and let the Supreme Intelligence rule. I had to keep reminding myself that the Higher Self does not always work quickly; it takes its time.

If your children have caused you pain, counseling or psychiatric sessions have not helped, and you finally realize that there is nothing you can do to help your children, let go and let the Supreme Intelligence rule. There are no better hands into which to place your children or your problems. Instead of trying to carry a crushing burden and having a nervous breakdown, release your problems, let go, and let the Supreme Intelligence rule. If your children are not a problem but you just want to keep them with you as long as possible, remember that holding on to children too long can create emotionally crippled adults who will be unable to make their own decisions.

Just as we tend to hold on to children too long, we may also try to remain in a love relationship that is not working. Ralph Waldo Emerson describes this experience: "If you put a chain around the neck of a slave, the other end fastens itself around your own." When you realize that a specific human being will not bend to your will, your desires, and your determination, cease the struggle. Start to release and let go; perfect good will come from this. The person you let go may not return to your life, but other persons will come into your life to fulfill you more abundantly. Take the risk and release your loved one—it will bring you freedom and happiness.

Some people form very close attachments to their parents; in the children's eyes, their parents can do no wrong. Even after they are married, have children, and run their own businesses, they remain children who need their mother's or father's approval. These perennial children make no changes in their lives unless their parents have ruled that these changes are right. When their parents die, these adult children are overcome by a terrible feeling of panic and self-punishment.

If you recognize yourself in this description, you need to release and let go of the particular relationship you have with your parent. Even if the parent is living, you need to do this. Proclaim your right as a person to hold your own thoughts and ideas; your concepts are just as good as your parent's ideas. Once you are free of your attachment to your parent, you will at last experience a freedom within yourself that you have never experienced before.

RELEASE YOURSELF THROUGH DETACHMENT

There was a time in my life when I said "no" to very few people. When I first started counseling people, I thought that I should be available for every human being. I gave money; I gave time and energy. Even though I was drained and tired, I gave more.

Then one day I discovered that the Infinite Intelligence gives each of us only so many people we are expected to take care of.

Are there people in your life whom you try to help or counsel but who will not listen? Then you have probably spent hours listening to their problems, trying to help them, even though they did not listen. They only wanted someone's ear, not caring what you had to say. The troubled speakers return but will never listen to what you are saying; they will drain you. Learn the lesson of detachment. You may want to help a lot of people, but you can only attach yourself to a few; you must detach the rest.

There are people who will pressure you into going to social functions when something inside you tells you that you do not want to go. How many times have you have gone to social events just to make someone else happy? Stop making everyone else happy—say *no*. Say *no* to people who waste your time and energy.

People who attach themselves to you are all part of the Supreme Intelligence, but the course on which they travel is different from yours. Discipline yourself so that you can stand up and say *no*. Only you can do that for yourself. When you say *no*, you will find that your friends will not be angry with you; they may be disappointed that you are not able to go, but they will still be your friends. And if your friends are not there for you tomorrow, it is possible that they are not supposed to be in your life. They may be preventing some good things from happening to you, especially if they continue to bombard you with negative ideas and negative thoughts. Maybe you need to lift yourself out of that condition. Listen to your Higher Self for guidance.

As you release these people and conditions in your life and let them go, your life expands and your thinking changes. Anytime that you let go of something, you will receive something new. Change always brings new things. If you can help people, then do so; but if you cannot help people, release them and let the Supreme Intelligence help them.

RELEASE YOUR WORRIES

Whenever I think of the Supreme Intelligence that created this earth, I am reminded of sowing a seed. Some of my happiest moments occurred when I took each of my children by the hand and helped him and her plant seeds and watched them grow. A week or so later, the seeds sprouted and blossomed into leaves. More leaves appeared and eventually a flower opened. Observing this act of nature is a wonderful way to teach children patience. By watching plants grow, they learn that it takes time for life to develop. With a little coaching from you, your children can apply this process to their own lives. The Supreme Intelligence did not create the earth quickly; it took many days, perhaps years.

If you often worry about the future, try to remember that varying amounts of time are needed for certain events in your life to unfold and these events are not affected in any way by worry. The Supreme Intelligence has everything in order and does not violate that order because each event is arranged. As we read in Proverbs, "To every thing there is a season, and a time to every purpose under the heaven." Do not waste your time and energy worrying about something that may never occur. Be forewarned: When you worry about something, your worry may draw that problem to you. Remind yourself frequently that the Infinite Intelligence has everything well in hand.

Some people are worried that the world may end tomorrow in a nuclear holocaust; others worry that in six months or a year from now something terrible will happen. Most of the things that people worry about will never happen. Think about it. The heads of companies who sell accident and fire insurance have thought about it; their statistical tables have proven that catastrophies do not happen as often as most people think they will. Worry has nothing to do with the future for insurance companies; they are certain that by insuring clients against accidents and fires, they can pay all claims and still make a profit.

Stop worrying about the future and what people say, or what you think they are going to say, about you. As a unique

85

human being, only you can control your own thoughts; why waste energy worrying about something over which you have no control? Do not worry about someone else's statements about politics, God, or church. Allow other people to have their own thoughts, ideas, dreams, desires, and feelings and they will allow you to have yours. Because each of us is a speck of that divine wonderful Higher Self, all of us have the right to attend the church of our choice, to vote for whomever we want, and to paint our houses purple if we so choose. Each of us has the right to make decisions, based on our different thoughts, feelings, ideas, and concepts. In the United States, this diversity has yielded a rich mix of cultures where we do not have to agree with everyone else; we have only to agree with the right of others to disagree with us.

RELEASE YOUR GUILT

Let go of your guilt and release those shameful things you have done in the past. Know that your Higher Self accepts you as you are. Do not condemn yourself for your past failures, affairs, or an unhappy marriage. Self-condemnation causes disease and illness. Release, let go, and let the Supreme Intelligence rule. Ask forgiveness for your failures; tears may come and your healing will have begun.

If guilt about a past act still hangs on in your life, you may not have been able to confess it or talk about it. You should know something right now: The Supreme Intelligence loves you right where you are, this very moment. Ask yourself: If you could have done anything other than what you did at the time, would you have done it? Was there a way for you to have done something differently? How did you think? How did you feel in your heart? What were the circumstances when you did it? Not that any of these feelings matter; the Supreme Intelligence loves you now because He knows that if you could have done anything other than what you did, you would have done it.

Looking back at your past life, if you can think of terrible things that you did to this child or to that person, you may need to seek forgiveness that you have not requested. If this is the case, ask forgiveness of those you have wronged and clean up that part of your life. Do not continually condemn yourself for past acts, because as long as these memories gnaw at you, you will never be free. You will be guilt-ridden all of your life and your health will reflect it. Pray and know that when you open yourself, the Infinite Intelligence hears you; at that moment you are perfect and whole. Cleanse yourself by using the releasing techniques on pages 92–93.

RELEASE YOUR FEARS

When I opened my counseling center, I introduced a practical way of eliminating health-threatening attachments to people and the fearful past. The group and I discussed death and dying and covered topics that those in the medical profession are unable to discuss with their patients because of lack of time. In disclosing our inner fears and sharing ideas, we found that, from very early childhood, most of us experience fear. Fear sometimes prevents very young children from meeting other children. Later in life, fear destroys any hope of building a future or even a peaceful life. From our discussions, we found that fear touched every human activity. When fear and pessimism interrelate in our bodies, the resulting stress causes mental and physical illness. Not only were some people in the group afraid of the outer world but many were afraid of their inner worlds. When I spoke of meditation, some people were afraid to go within themselves and sit in silence. (Meditation will be discussed in Chapter 8.)

While fear has sent people to mental hospitals, a lot of those on the outside live with debilitating phobias, obsessions, and compulsions in their everyday lives. Like a well-cut diamond, fear has many facets: One person may experience claustrophobia in an elevator or small room; another may be afraid of being alone. Once I counseled a man who sometimes left abruptly because his wife was afraid to be alone in their house. His wife's fears prevented him from accepting a higher-salaried job as a traveling salesman. Fear barricades some people within their houses; they cannot step outside the door for fear of being hurt by others. People who have phobias such as these usually suffer from excessive fear in the absence of real danger.

Some timid souls hesitate about everything in life. Afraid to make the wrong decision, they hesitate fearfully for months before deciding to buy a coat or go to a doctor. Some sick people are afraid to be operated on because they fear that they will die during the operation. One of the greatest fears is the fear of death: As much as we want to be with the Supreme Intelligence, we are fearful of dying in order to get there.

A cleaning fanatic may run himself ragged to calm his fears that everything is not perfectly clean. Other compulsive people have ritualized ways of dressing or undressing, brushing their teeth, getting up in the morning, and doing chores. People with compulsive obsessions were most likely reared by dominating, strong-willed, or severely disciplined parents. Very early in that person's life, someone made him feel unworthy and fearful of being with others.

Important changes in our lives may trigger fears. It would be unusual to feel no anxiety when starting a new venture or a new job. On one hand, we want to go too fast, and on the other, we are tempted to slow down. When starting something new, fear can cause us to seek excuses that short-circuit our possibilities for success. This is exemplified in the case of a mother who allowed her daughter to climb trees. Then, remembering that the boy next door had fallen out of a tree onto his head, she became so anxious about her child's safety that she commanded the girl to come down.

There are people who consistently opt for failure instead of success. A woman I counseled wanted to know why her husband always failed as soon as he reached the point at which he could have been successful. I told her that he must have had a fear of

doing wrong. We traced his fear back to his childhood; h
were very strict about his earning outstanding grades in
It was so important to them that he get all A's that he
considered a failure if he did not. Even though he tried hard,
could not attain perfect grades. When he came home with a C,
his father reprimanded him and grounded him for over a month, saying that he should try harder to get that A. The boy stopped trying because every time he got close to success, he thought he would still fail—he would try only so far and stop. Once he found out what negative programming his subconscious had acquired in childhood, he changed his thinking and began to take risks. Now he could take the risk of failing, knowing that when he tried, even though he failed, he was still a winner.

Fear and suspicion overshadow the world. Our only hope is that no matter who you are or what religion or race you belong to, you have a desire to find happiness. Part of this desire is that your children will grow up in a secure world with futures better than your own. Do not let your desires for your children cause tension and anxiety. You survived and they will, too.

Start to examine your fears and anxieties; you may find that they have been caused by past experiences that you had forgotten. Look at each fear so that you can learn to live with it. If, for example, you find it difficult to take responsibility and to make decisions, your anxiety and fear could be rooted in an overprotected childhood. Go back to your childhood, recognize where your fears came from, and be certain that this negative programming in your subconscious mind can be reprogrammed.

Fears can be conquered when you recognize them for what they are and know that they can be conquered. Look at yourself as a human being who has the right to live in happiness and peace, not in fear. Refuse to be motivated by the fear of what others may think of you. The criticism of negative people does not matter because you have a right to your own thinking and your own way of living. You have been created by the Supreme Intelligence in His image. Say affirmations often to confirm this in your life.

fears now seem irrational and nonsensical
~ears you have probably forgotten the orig-
~g that happened to you as a child. Break
y that someone else may have had over
ur daily life; be courageous and positive
on your fears; be sure to track down the
~e you do these things, you are going to
~nd begin to live successfully. Remember
~~~~ you have a right to be happy.

RELEASE YOUR INSECURITY

If you say things such as "I'm no good" or "I'm not worth
anything," you are full of insecurity based on negative programming from the past. When you realize that you have been rejecting yourself as something worthless, you will know that you have
been damaging a good person. Know that you have a right to
achieve and that you are valuable. You are a child of the Infinite
Intelligence and you must do well for yourself on this earth.

You can diminish your feelings of insecurity by beginning
to do small things that bring you success instead of failure. In
this way, you will be able to replace your feelings of insecurity
with feelings of success. If you happen to be in a relationship or
circumstances that are contributing to your insecurity, then you
have to change that environment. If you are living with someone
who causes you to feel like a failure or if you are working at a
job that makes you feel that way, you may need to speak to a
counselor or friend. After you get a proper perspective on it, alter
the situation. Do not remain in a situation that smothers your
success; do something to remedy that situation. Otherwise, you
are going to start worrying about failure again. Know that you
will succeed; believe that you can do it; hold onto that belief and
you will be successful.

RELEASE YOUR SELF-PITY

Oh, those terrible, terrible self-pity feelings! No one wants to be around a person who is full of self-pity. Self-pity virtually encases the one who pities within himself. Although he does not understand why, he isolates himself from people by telling everyone in great detail about his problems.

During one of my workshops, a young lady explained that she had had a happy childhood. Forty-five minutes later, she raised her hand and said, "Well, I do not want you to think that my childhood was *that* happy because I really had this terrible thing happen to me and I want to tell you . . ." This person lives in self-pity; it was evident that the rest of the group did not want to hear what she was saying because she wanted so desperately to get their attention and earn their sympathy. She probably did not receive enough attention when she was a child.

Until you are able to release self-pity from your life, you will not find happiness. The first step is to recognize that you have this condition; then find out what you can do to change it. Begin by thanking your Higher Self for where you are. Have gratitude for the blessings that you have received because with the bad there is some good. Changing your attitude toward the condition causing your self-pity does not mean that you are accepting it but rather that you are changing your mind's attitude toward it and refusing to feel self-pity.

Laugh Away Your Self-Pity. We need more laughter in our lives but laughter is not always easy to find. We need more Flip Wilsons and fewer Jack the Rippers. Newspapers feature only one page of comics; the other pages feature many gruesome stories of violence and crime. News telecasts have the same ratio of funny stories to sad, wrapping up their thirty minutes of mayhem with a token human-interest story. Commercials and advertisements feed us messages with dire warnings about everything from headaches or hemorrhoids to cemetery plots.

91

If you look for the humor of life, you will find it. Start with yourself; recall all the crazy, humorous moments of your life. Regardless of the source, if you enjoy fifteen minutes of laughter each day, you will have good health and less time for self-pity.

Norman Cousins' experience proves the power of laughter.* When his doctor told Cousins that he had only one chance in 500 of surviving a connective tissue disease, Cousins refused to die. Taking charge of his own recovery, he moved from the hospital to a more restful hotel room. He found that not only was staying at the hotel less expensive, but the food was better. The hotel also afforded him the privacy to watch Candid Camera films and Marx Brothers movies whenever he wished. In addition to the films, friends read humorous books aloud. Cousins beat the odds with chuckles, belly laughs, and Vitamin C.

While you are wallowing in self-pity, read stories written by people who have triumphed over their own conditions, such as *Karen* and *Don't Fall off the Mountain*. Think of the blind, crippled, and orphaned children in the war-torn Middle East or the starving families in Africa. Read the evening newspaper and you will not have difficulty finding conditions that are worse than your own. In addition to reading, keep your mind occupied so that there is no time to think about how terrible your condition is. In the next few pages, I will be saying more about accepting difficulties in life.

RELEASING TECHNIQUE

Find a quiet place and sit in silence. Surrender the angry feelings that you have kept; release those grievances, fears, and worries. After you have thought of all the people who have brought harm to you, bless them. Ask the Supreme Intelligence to bless each

*Norman Cousins, *Anatomy of an Illness, as Perceived by the Patient* (New York: W. W. Norton & Company, 1979).

of them with prosperity and love and happiness. Forgive the.
for hurting you and forgive yourself for the things that you may
have done to cause them to hurt you. You may want to use the
affirmation "I am free from all resentments, from all people in
all places, and from all things. In my past and present, I have
no room for resentment because love fills me through and
through."

LETTER-TO-THE-SUPREME-INTELLIGENCE TECHNIQUE

One of the most rewarding techniques I have used is writing to
the Supreme Intelligence. After addressing Him, "Dear Supreme
Intelligence," I tell how heavily burdened I am and that I am
releasing all the negative things that have happened in my life
to Him. At the end of the letter, I thank Him for taking care of
this for me. Then, without rereading the letter, I stuff all of the
pages into a bucket, set them on fire, and flush the ashes down
the toilet. Thoughts of negativity have been released and the
Supreme Intelligence has taken care of them.

When you use this technique, remember not to reread what
you have written. By rereading your letter, you send these thoughts
out into the universe again; just burn the letter. Your Higher
Self will cleanse you.

ANGELS IN DISGUISE

Many times, different experiences are given to us so that we
might learn from these experiences. Dr. Robert Schuller has said
that liabilities can be turned into assets and that seemingly negative experiences may be angels in disguise. I have seen this
transformation from bad to good in people who are ill. I would
not have known my life's mission had I not become so ill that I

go on welfare to survive. My rheumatoid arthritis ⎯ me to use the powers of my subconscious and to ⎯ he Supreme Intelligence rule.

⎯ vant to affirm when trouble starts, "This trouble ⎯periencing cannot hurt me; it will help me; it is going to make me a finer person and I will have a better character because of it. I am going to look at this problem in the right spirit and I will do what I need to do to get through this experience in the right way. Because of it, I am going to be able to help other people with similar problems."

So often when I am counseling other people, I am able to use my own experiences as guidelines. If you are to be of help to humanity, then you must first dip your feet in this earth to feel pain and to suffer. When trouble comes to you, do not sit back, idle. Do something! As long as you take action, you will not have time to become filled with self-pity when you think and rethink the situation. Visit people in hospitals and nursing homes; listen to their problems and refrain from telling them yours. Visit lonely neighbors—help them with their yardwork or take them to the store. Offer to baby-sit for young parents who need some time for themselves. By doing charitable things like these, you will find that as you give, you will receive.

If your life has been filled with disappointment and bitterness, you may feel that you have lost your faith. At one time, I thought I had lost my faith, too. I believe that no one actually loses faith but that we either never had it or we misplace it temporarily. If you have misplaced your faith, pray as though you believe and you *will* believe. Matthew 7:7 said, "Ask, and it will be given you; seek and you will find; knock and it will be opened to you. For everyone who asks, receives; and he who seeks, finds; and to him who knocks, it will be opened." Each day, affirm that, "Faith is mine. My life is prosperous, my spouse is loving, my children are giving, and I am loving." Eventually, through that kind of faith, good things will manifest in your life and you will start to see results.

94

TURNING LIABILITIES INTO ASSETS

After you have asked your Higher Self to change your old attitudes and purify your being, you may still experience heartaches and other burdens. Thinking positively every waking minute is not easy; neither is removing resentment or hate within your heart. Continuing to purify your body of old habits, old thought patterns, and old concepts is very difficult. Just when you think that you have it all together, somebody will test you to see if you have really mastered this new way of life.

This was my test: I once shared a financial venture with two of my students. One day, my partners decided to leave; they took with them all the people that we had brought together as a group and the business was dissolved. When people said that what they had done to me was awful, I responded that they were good people but needed to experience what they were doing. I did not talk badly about either of them, but it was a painful experience. I had lost a lot of money and they had taken almost all of my clients. Eighteen months later, when my new enterprise began to show profits, I learned that their business had failed.

Before I learned about the powers of the subconscious, I did not know why I was so miserable or when I was experiencing a lesson—all I knew was that the situation was horrible. Now when I experience pain, I look around and search my soul, asking, "What am I experiencing? What have I drawn toward myself? What am I in need of learning?" I may not like the experience and even though I may cry, I know that with the blackness of night the light comes and in that light is truth and peace and a wholeness of spirit. I know that with tomorrow's light there will be faith reborn in me, a lesson learned, and that the light of my Higher Self will shine even more abundantly in me.

Teachers in ancient civilizations knew that humans need to learn some lessons here on earth. The saints knew they had to go through a cleansing. Each of us has a consciousness that must be cleansed: We can affirm at any time: "O Higher Self, purify me; create in me a clean heart; renew in me a right spirit." Know that when you say those words, you will receive trials and tribulations that will cleanse you—your outside world must change so that your inside world can change. Both must be cleansed and purified.

When you experience any kind of unhappiness, look at the situation and ask what you are learning from this experience. How does it contribute to your growth or understanding? How must you live today? What good is it showing you? Each time a problem arises (losing money, going through a divorce, or losing a loved one), you are being presented with a lesson. This lesson is a learning experience that will purify you—it is an experience for the soul. Sometimes those experiences are blessings.

Why is it that a woman will marry an alcoholic, divorce him, swear never to look at another alcoholic, and then marry another? This person will repeat this pattern until she learns a lesson: She is drawing to herself what she fears. She will continue to draw the same lessons to herself until she no longer fears that condition and learns compassion, love, and understanding. When it is no longer necessary to hold on to the fear, she can release it and go on with her life. People in this situation do not find love, compassion, and understanding; instead, they find more hate and resentment. And they continue to attract what they fear.

Frequently, those habits that we dislike so much in other people are the very same ones we dislike in ourselves. Be willing to learn from both your loved ones and from strangers. Let each person become your teacher. Remind yourself, "I am ready to learn again. What is this person going to teach me?" Once you learn the lesson, truly know it, or the same personality with a different face will appear again in your life and you will be presented with the same kind of problems. After you have learned from a previous experience, you will be able to release the problem when it presents itself again. If you find that bad experiences continually occur in your life, you are still drawing the same problems to yourself. Once you have learned the lesson, you will not draw the same problem.

Now that you have gotten rid of your anger, resentment, guilt, and hate from the past, you are on your way to becoming a new creation. The next chapter is about prayer; it will help you become closer to your Higher Self in this wonderful change.

SEVEN

Pray Always

When a little boy was asked, "Who made you?" he answered, "God made me, but I grew the rest myself." Each of us must take responsibility for "growing the rest" of ourselves. This involves taking full responsibility for reeducating our subconscious minds by learning to pray properly, sit in silence, meditate, and affirm. The Bible says that we are what we think in our hearts: If we change our thoughts through prayer and meditation, our hearts and then our lives will change because the desires of our hearts are incorporated into our subconscious minds.

Only prayer can change your character. When that change happens, you will become a very different person. Some people consider this change a conversion because there is such a drastic transformation that the person is truly born again. Saul's conversion on the road to Damascus reveals how life-shattering this change can be. Do not regard prayer as the simple pastime of the very young or the very old—prayer can change your character and your life.

FORGIVE BEFORE YOU PRAY

Before prayer can change your character, you must forgive others and then forgive yourself. The love of your Higher Self cannot enter a bitter, unforgiving heart that is full of resentment. Use the releasing techniques in Chapter 6 to rid yourself of these negative emotions. If after trying these techniques there is still someone you have not been able to forgive, try imagining that you are talking to that person from your past (select a time and place where you will be neither disturbed nor overheard). Imagine that the person is standing before you; accuse this person of all the wrongs you have stored up all these years. If you need a physical release, scream or beat a pillow. Feel the pain of rejection or hatred one final time; then forgive the person and release that person forever. Many times during this cathartic process, you will gain new insights into what happened in the past and why. You may find that a particular suffering in your past prepared you to face problems later on.

Once your spirit has been purified by forgiveness, remember to pray with sincerity. If your heart is troubled, you do not have peace, you have fear of some type, and there is resentment, then you will not receive what you ask for in prayer. Remove these remnants of the past so that they cannot interfere with your sincere concentration.

HOW TO PRAY

Remember that Jesus did not teach details; He taught principles—in this case, the principle that we should pray. How each of us accomplishes this is up to our individual creativity and spontaneity. Therefore, while I can offer suggestions about prayer based on my own experiences and learning, the details of how to pray are really up to you.

Pray as you are led to pray by the desire that comes from within you. Prayer is more than asking for something you wish

to attain; it is attuning yourself to a definite po
pray, place your mind and spirit in the spiritual
All things can be created in the spiritual realn
truly creative. Remember that you are praying
God or Higher Self, not a distant God some
Before you begin praying, take a few deep brea...
erately relax your mind and body. Attune yourself to the forces
of the universe within you.

Four questions are commonly asked about prayer. The first
is "Should I pray to God directly or through a particular saint
or my guardian angel?" Always pray to the Supreme Intelligence
as a loving father to whom you can speak directly. You may
share your ideas, dreams, and desires with your favorite saint or
your teachers in spirit, but pray only to your indwelling God.
Often, God will answer your prayer by allowing the answer
to manifest through those guardian angels who know your
desires.

The second question is "Should I sit or kneel during prayer?"
If kneeling helps your focus your thoughts on the Supreme Intel-
lect, then kneel. If your arthritic knees complain when you kneel,
by all means sit. If you sit all day and would rather stand, do
that. If you can stay awake, you can certainly pray while lying
down. Your Higher Self listens, regardless of your posture.

A third question is "What prayers should I use when I
pray?" Most frequently, your prayer will be a spontaneous outpouring from your heart and soul to your indwelling God. This
may be a brief "Help!" or a grateful "Thank you," or a longer
prayer; the length of the prayer depends on the circumstances.
Whether you pray silently or aloud also depends on where and
when you pray.

At various times, you may abandon spontaneous prayer to
seek the comfort of the Lord's Prayer or the psalms: The Bible
contains the greatest prayers ever written. After choosing a
psalm—Psalm 23, for example—read it slowly many times, paus-
ing frequently to become receptive to inspiration. Another psalm
you may want to use is Psalm 46, which will enable you to

come any kind of difficulty. (Chapter 9 lists other psalms that can be used as prayers in various situations.)

A fourth question I am frequently asked is "Should I pray with others or by myself?" There is no general rule for this: If you can pray with more fervor with a prayer partner, then do so. Most people find that praying in a group increases their feelings and awareness, so they pray with a group whenever possible. You will recall that Jesus asked His followers to pray with Him on the Mount of Olives.

The most important thing about prayer is to pray with everything you have: Feel it, believe it, expect what you are praying for to manifest. Then let go and let the Supreme Intelligence rule, whether you are praying by yourself or with others. Catherine Ponder suggests that you pray the way you make love—with everything you've got!

Pray Daily. Prayer should be a continuous practice involving all aspects of your life, whether large or small. Learn to pray not as a duty or only when you are in trouble, but when you can talk to God as you would a friend. Tell Him your needs, desires, and joys; remember to thank Him frequently for your many blessings. Let your prayers be a spontaneous outpouring of your heart and soul. Set aside a specific time each day—just ten minutes—to talk with your Higher Self. You will find that, as Jesus said, "All things whatsoever ye shall ask in prayer, believe and ye shall receive."

Because prayer is rooted in the law of love, you will find that the more frequently you give of yourself, the more frequently will the things you are praying for become a reality in your life. Prayer asks and love grants according to how much you have given. Your prayer will be answered only to the measure of rewards earned through your thoughts, service to others, and how much you have donated. When you give, you invest your treasures; when you receive, you withdraw from your storehouse. If you expect the help of angels in obtaining your desires and prayers, be an angel to others.

While you are learning to pray, learn to live one day at a time. As the psalmist said, this is the day the Lord has made—be thankful and rejoice. Ask God to give you what you need for the next twenty-four hours, just for today. Let your enthusiasm in prayer spill into your life; throughout the day, enjoy each moment. Each person who enters your life this day will become special, someone to be enjoyed.

Pray for Everyone. Take a few minutes each day to pray for your brothers and sisters all over the world. The Supreme Intelligence has made all of us members of one another. John states in the Bible "I am the vine, you are the branches. He who remains in me, and I in him, bears much fruit. For apart from me you can do nothing." Our world has been made less than perfect by the errors of our human family. Prayer can help those who suffer the loss of home, family, or livelihood because of these errors.

Pray especially for those who, through some misunderstanding, are against you or desire to harm you. Pray for those who give to you. Remember what I said about receiving in Chapter 4: Although it is better to give than to receive, someone has to receive to bless those who give. Tell God how truly thankful you are for those who give to you.

Pray for those who have left this world. Many times, your prayers for a loved one who has died may help that spirit move into another dimension. This is important because that soul may need to go to another dimension in order to continue learning.

Pray for Yourself. Praying for yourself is not selfish. Asking for guidance, wisdom, understanding, or health will enable you to help others. You are helpless to help others if your own well is dry or you are burned out. As I suggested in Chapter 5, do a little soul searching. Reach deep down inside yourself and ask what you need to pray about. What has your Higher Self planned for you as a person? What kind of career or interests should you pursue? Anything is possible—the Infinite Intelligence has a plan for everyone. If you discover the very thing you are intended to do, you will be able to remove all the obstacles in your path and start to see success in your life. Pray that this secret desire of your heart will be revealed to you. When you allow that to manifest in your life, you will become happy and secure because for the first time, you will find your true place in life.

The state of your soul is always expressed in your outward appearance. Ralph Waldo Emerson said, "What you are stands over you the while, and thunders so that I cannot hear what you say to the contrary." When you live a life full of prayer, your surroundings and life will shine. You will not have to shout your spiritual truth to others. When there is peace and joy in you, others will want to share your world. People will invite themselves to become a part of your life.

As your life begins to change and you experience prayer that is working, you will find that your life will be purer, truer, and less selfish than it has ever been before. You will have more love in your heart than you have ever experienced in your life. This is the test that tells you things are starting to change. You will find that spiritual development is a matter of growth, and because growth takes time, spiritual development is a gradual process. The law of the universe has its own rhythm: A flower takes time to grow, a sun takes time to rise, and leaves take time, to develop on the trees. Do not hasten your spiritual growth; allow your soul to be nurtured by time as you pray for your development.

Pray with Feeling. Prayers should be spontaneous rather than repetitious. When your prayers are spontaneous, you will pray with feeling and be more receptive to divine inspiration. Go to your Higher Self as you would to a senior business partner: Be definite and precise. Lay everything out on the table; state exactly what you want. Jesus was not a vague man; He stated what He wanted and asked for what He wanted. As you are praying and visualizing what you desire, remember that the Infinite Intelligence will give you what you need.

If you find that your mind is distracted while you are saying an affirmation and visualizing what you desire, stop saying your affirmations and do whatever you were thinking about—paying the bills, doing the laundry, and so on. Return later when you are able to concentrate on your Higher Self and resume your prayer with a fresh mind and a full heart. After you have mastered the concentration techniques featured in the next chapter, you will no longer have this problem of concentration.

Pray with Confidence. Believe that you will receive whatever you ask for in prayer. Do you pray to God for something and soon after think that you are not worthy of it? If you do, your prayer will not be answered. As a child of the Higher Self within you, you are worthy. You must get in touch with your indwelling presence. Get in tune with your Higher Self and when you pray, remember that the Supreme Intelligence's will for you is for greater freedom and expression, good health, and all the wonderful things you can imagine. Know that as you pray, whatever you pray for is yours; remember that God knows what you desire before you ask. Know that if you are in harmony with God's will, those things that you pray for will come into your life.

WHAT WE EXPECT, WE EXPERIENCE

Priests in ancient temples administered drugs and hypnotic suggestions to their patients before the patients went to sleep. The priests told them that the gods would visit them in their sleep and heal them. Many healings followed this and the patients went forth praising the gods.

In the twentieth century, a doctor began selling healing sticks in a certain town. He told people that these healing sticks were blessed and held great powers. Miraculous healings began happening. The doctor did a landslide business in healing sticks because people were healed. In the midst of this, a newspaper headline charged that the doctor was a fake. The article stated that the police had searched the doctor's warehouse and found thousands of ordinary sticks. The next day, as the doctor sat in jail awaiting trial for fraud, all of the people who had been miraculously healed gradually became sick again.

One day while I was reading Catherine Ponder's book, *Pray and Grow Rich*,* a woman approached me and said with a slightly self-righteous sniff, "Oh, isn't that something; now we can pray for selfish things." I answered, "In this book, *rich* means to be rich in health and love and to be prosperous in our ways because this is what God our Father wants for us." The woman looked at me with uncertainty and then joined me. Forty-five minutes later, she walked away with a smile on her face, mentioning that she intended to buy the book. I hope that after reading the book, she was able to pray with the confidence of a child requesting her inheritance.

Pray with Persistence. If I feel deep inside of me that something is badly needed, I persist in my prayers. The need could be a home for a homeless child, money that I need to pay salaries, or rent money. I insist when I am very much in need. I go to my Higher Self many times a day, saying, "Listen to me, God; here I am, again. I need, O God." And it is given because, like Isaac and Abraham in the Old Testament who prayed for more than twenty years, I insist and persist.

If there is an emergency situation and you need something immediately, pray more often. Pray in silence and talk aloud to your High Self, as you would to a friend. Even while praying persistently, pray in complete freedom, realizing that the Supreme Intelligence will give you what He knows you need, not what you think you want. I found this out the hard way.

At one time in my life, I prayed for a house that I felt should be mine. I prayed for six months feeling I really needed that house very badly. Well, I did not get it, even after all those

*Catherine Ponder, *Pray and Grow Rich* (Englewood Cliffs, N.J.: Prentice-Hall, Inc., 1968).

prayers and tears. Although I had outlined to God exactly how I should receive the house, I did not receive it. I am thankful I did not receive that house because soon after someone else bought it, the house was destroyed when the furnace blew up. If I had bought that house, my family might have been killed. Two months later God gave me and my family a most wonderful place to live, much nicer than the house I had prayed for. The lesson I learned was that God did not give me what I thought I wanted; my heavenly father gave me what He knew I needed. This is how I learned to pray for God's will in a situation, even while I persistently storm heaven.

TESTING PRAYER

Many times we ask God for direction in our lives, and yet we do not always hear His answer. The next time this happens, you may wish to use the fleece system that Gideon used in the Bible. When Gideon did not know the direction that God wanted him to take and could not hear God's voice, he asked God to give him a sign that he could understand. Gideon said to God, "Prove it to me this way: I'll put a fleece on the threshing floor tonight and in the morning if the fleece is wet and the ground is dry, I will know you are going to help me." And it happened just that way! When he got up the next morning, the fleece was wet and the ground was dry. Yet, Gideon wanted to make sure he was going in the right direction and that the test was accurate. He said to God, "Please don't be angry with me, but let me make one more test. This time let the fleece remain dry while the ground around it is wet." So the Lord did as He was asked; that night the fleece stayed dry, but the ground was covered with dew! Gideon knew that God was speaking to him and was able to go in the right direction.

You, too, can ask for a sign as Gideon did in the Old Testament. Perhaps you need an answer in two weeks: Begin to take action about whatever is to manifest in your life. As you recall from Chapter 6, you must release the old to make room for the new; create a vacuum to receive an answer to your prayer. If what you are praying for is right for you, every door will be opened for you and what you requested will flow in. If what you desire is not right for you, every door will be closed and you will know—or you *should* know. So many times, people try to force open doors blocked by obstacles, and failure results. For example, people may ask for a sign about buying a certain house but, even after having trouble obtaining a clear title, they persist; when they have trouble getting financing, they persist. Later, when they are sitting in a house that is not right for them, they wonder, "Why didn't my Higher Self guide me?"

Whenever you want to know the truth about a situation or a person, ask for a sign. If you are thinking about leaving your church and looking for a new church or if you are thinking of marrying someone, ask your heavenly Father what the truth of the matter is. Ask your Higher Self to guide you and show you the way.

GOD ANSWERS ALL PRAYERS

All prayers are answered. They are answered within the time-frame created by divine law. Some prayers are answered quickly if what you have prayed for is harmonious with your life; other prayers require slower action. Then there are those prayers that appear to be ignored, when the answer is actually *No* or *Maybe*: Sometimes this happens because you have left it to Providence and did not take action yourself, such as releasing the old to make room for the new. At other times, your Higher Self knew that what you were praying for was not in your best interest at that time. In this case, your request may be put on a "back burner" until the time is right for you to receive your request. If you need to grow before receiving your request, a good start is to rid yourself of negative emotions. The Infinite Intelligence will wait until you are ready to receive your request, for He determines the order of the universe.

Many times when people do not receive what they pray for, they think that their prayers have not been answered. Actually, the Supreme Intelligence answered their prayers but not with the answers they were looking for. If someone prays that she wins millions of dollars in a lottery and is given an idea worth millions, her prayer has been answered but not in the way she imagined. A good way to pray for a change in circumstances or a specific object is to ask that what you are requesting brings contentment to all concerned in attaining your desires. Remember, if receiving what you prayed for necessitated depriving another of that circumstance or object, attaining your prayer now may decrease your happiness later.

No matter what your Higher Self's answer to your prayer is, be prepared. Build up your trust to the point where you can realize that a *No* means what you want is not what you need. This is another time to let go and let the Supreme Intelligence rule. Remember Jesus' prayer at the Mount of Olives: "not my will but thine be done." Increase your patience so that when the time is not yet right to fulfill your request or you need to grow in some aspect of your life, you can endure cheerfully until you receive your request. Strengthen your faith in your Higher Self so that you can use what you prayed for to God's honor and glory; in other words, be prepared to receive what you requested. This is not always easy, as the following story from Catherine Ponder's book, *Pray and Grow Rich*,* illustrates. A Catholic girl fell in love with and wished to marry a Protestant boy. Because they came from different religious backgrounds, the girl asked her mother to pray with her concerning the situation. So both of them prayed.

The first week that they prayed, the young fellow she wanted to marry passed by the Catholic church she attended. This encouraged the young woman and her mother, so they continued

---

*Catherine Ponder, *Pray and Grow Rich* (Englewood Cliffs, N.J.: Prentice-Hall, Inc., 1968).

praying. The second week, he not only passed by the church but this time he looked in. The third week, they prayed and prayed; not only did the young man look in, but this time he went inside and sat down. The mother and daughter continued to pray.

The fourth week, as the women's hopes and dreams were ready to be answered and their prayers were mounting, the young man told the young girl that he had talked to her priest. This made her very happy. The fifth week, he announced that he had decided to join her church. The sixth week of prayer for this young man brought a big surprise. The girl sobbed to her mother, "Oh, Mama, we prayed too hard; now he's going to be a priest."

This story dramatizes that sometimes we pray so hard that what we pray for works in reverse; we get our request, but it is more than we bargained for. This means that we did not realize the full scope of our request when we began praying. It also shows that we need to relax more when we pray, to let go and let the Supreme Intelligence rule. My sister Wanda once affirmed that she would make 350 dollars a week in her home decoration business. Months later, she had booked many parties in order to sell her products and the business came to her. People called to request that she give parties at their homes. Even though she had enlisted the help of my mother and stepfather to unpack and check her products, she was working eighteen hours a day and falling farther and farther behind in her work. She soon discovered that there are sacrifices to be made for wishes to come true. Be prepared to get what you ask for.

Recently, when a small southern town was suffering from a drought, the mayor, who was also the minister, called the townspeople together in the church to pray for rain. They prayed and prayed; then they sang and prayed. Suddenly, they heard the pitter-patter of rain hitting the roof and saw gentle drops streaking the church windows. They ran out and kissed the earth, thanking God for the rain. As the gentle rain turned into a downpour, the townspeople returned to the church for shelter and projected how long they would have to wait for the rain to stop so they could return to their homes without getting drenched.

110

All the while, standing shyly near the door of the church was a six-year-old girl with an umbrella—the only one in the crowd who truly believed that it would rain. Again, be prepared to get what you ask for.

USE A PRAYER WHEEL

I use a prayer wheel often in my daily life—the results are outstanding. As you can see from Figure 2, a prayer wheel is very easy to create. You can use this wheel to go from your heart to your consciousness to your Higher Self; let what you desire start to manifest for you. Complete your prayer wheel over a period of time, not in one day. Place what you desire, or the result of what you desire, in the center. Each spoke is a positive thought about what you want. You may add as many spokes as you wish, but you should add only one spoke each day.

Beneath your prayer wheel, write a positive affirmation such as, "I am perfect for the job. It is in divine order and my Higher Self is with me. All is in harmony." Concentrate on your prayer wheel for fifteen minutes before going to bed. Think about your affirmation; visualize it, feel it, know that you will receive what you want if it is in the Supreme Intelligence's plan. When you are not using your prayer wheel, keep it hidden so that the negative vibrations of others cannot affect your desire.

Pray silently when you use a prayer wheel. Do not discuss the subject of your prayer wheel with others because their negative thoughts could prevent your desire from being manifested. Discussing your desire also dissipates your idea into the universe; other people's random thoughts scatter your idea throughout the universe rather than centering all energies on the idea.

The art of imagination comes into play when you use a prayer wheel. If you are not well, you will want to picture yourself in your mind's eye as healthy and whole while you are using your prayer wheel. If your debts outweigh your checkbook, picture the money that you need and see yourself paying bills with

111

Affirmation: My book is being published. It is in divine order and God is with me. All is in harmony.

Figure 2. A prayer wheel. Spend at least fifteen minutes each day thinking about your prayer and reading your affirmation.

it. By imagining what you are concentrating on, you are able to generate more energies to be released to God; this helps manifest the things that you desire.

MY ANSWERED PRAYER

I endured a very difficult time before I started to write this book. My work load had doubled and I was struggling helplessly for an answer but wasn't getting anywhere. I prayed and called a

112

prayer partner to ask if she would pray with me. Yet I was not able to free myself. As the week wore on, I became more desperate. I kept praying for the right thoughts and for the right decrees to use.

My Higher Self answered my prayer in the form of a book by Dr. Robert Schuller, *Living Positively One Day at a Time.** Opening the book, I was greeted by a miracle: On the first page, I read that anyone being led into a vital and exciting life filled with new possibilities and dynamic potential could be enthusiastic today about tomorrow. This was the very thing that was happening to me. I was being led into a new, exciting life. Why was I running from this exciting situation? Why could I not become more enthusiastic? My life had started to change; my horizons were expanding. I had been offered a weekly television show in my city and a cable television series to boot.

Finally, I realized that while I had been doing a lot of spiritual thinking, there was still a lot of fear in me—not fear of success but fear of losing the inner peace that I had worked so hard to establish. With Dr. Schuller's affirmation that a fantastic tomorrow was waiting for me, I began to look ahead positively. I wrote my dreams and commitments down in his book. After only a few months, these dreams began to manifest in my life. I recommend Dr. Schuller's book to anyone who is seeking as I was; it gave me the strength to return to my life and begin my future.

Now that I have given you my ideas about prayer, which is a time of asking, I am going to teach you how to meditate because meditation is a time of receiving.

*Robert Schuller, *Living Positively One Day at a Time* (Old Tappan, N.J.: Fleming Revell Co., 1981).

EIGHT

Listen to the Small, Still Voice

Take time to be in the presence of your Higher Self each day; set aside a special time to be able to hear what the prophet Elijah described as a small, still voice. Make an appointment with your Higher Self for thirty minutes a day; after you have learned to meditate, you will find that your problems have faded away. You will not experience the anger, impatience, depression, or fear that you once had. After attaining clearer insight, you will be able to let go of the trivial things and begin removing the clutter from your life.

DISCOVER THE ART OF LISTENING TO GOD

I discovered the powers of meditation quite by accident. I had been in the habit of praying but with little confidence. I was used to asking but not used to listening. Then one day I was sitting in a chair feeling very down because of my constant pain; I was depressed and lonely. Suddenly, I began to pray, talking to my Higher Self very quietly. Because I felt like crying, I took a few deep breaths, knowing that sometimes a deep breath will hold back the tears. While I was praying, I inhaled and held my breath and released it slowly until I felt more relaxed.

Then I noticed a feeling of warmth in my rib cage—it felt good! Had I contacted my Higher Self? I closed my eyes and learned the greatest lesson that I have ever learned: The reason that God gave us two ears and one mouth. I stopped talking and listened. At first there was nothing but silence; then I experienced a warmth that went from the top of my head to the tips of my toes. I felt all the heaviness on my shoulders lifted from me. I was barely breathing but I could hear my breath gently going in and out.

With each breath I took, more peace flowed into my body. I felt a clearing away of the negative feelings that I had had when I sat down. My chest and heart were filled with a wonderful feeling of perfect peace. Feeling renewed, I went into a very slight meditation, into a state of nothingness. I could hear my breathing, and for the first time, I was conscious of knowing more than what is seen and heard. My Higher Self, my intuitive self, came alive; I began to know more about the past, the present, and the future.

Every day I would go back and sit in that same room. I learned to wait, to experience the calmness, and to listen to an inner voice speak to me. No human voice could ever tell me what I learned at that time. Inner growth began in that stillness and a power was released in me. As I breathed each breath, I knew that the Infinite Intelligence was part of each breath and I felt Him fill my being. Just as Adam became a living soul when God breathed the breath of life into his nostrils, so did I. I had been dead to my inner world, but now I was alive.

Day after day, I returned to that moment of quietness and the feeling of divine love that I experienced, a warmth that penetrated my whole being. Each time I left that room, I was filled with a desire to help other people. When I wondered how I could do more than I was doing, I was given an answer. My spiritual consciousness awakened and I felt the way the apostles must have felt when Jesus awakened them by breathing on them, saying, "Receive ye the Holy Spirit."

Once I learned how to relax, the tension in my body vanished and I was able to meditate. Previously, I had been so tense when I prayed that I could not pray with confidence; this in turn caused failure. Gradually, a healing affected my mind, body, and spirit. That healing evolved from this relaxed state because I was drawing only positive forces to myself. At the same time, I was releasing from my consciousness all of my problems, concerns, and doubts; this allowed the universal wisdom and mind to flow in and through me.

Before I teach you what I have learned about the art of meditation, I will discuss two concentration techniques and the white-light technique that you must practice before you actually begin meditating. You will be using these techniques to concentrate and invoke the white light while you are meditating.

CONCENTRATION TECHNIQUES

To meditate, the first thing you have to learn is to concentrate. Centering your mind on one particular idea may not be easy for you since you are accustomed to dealing with all the details of daily life. Even though concentration is not easy, with discipline, you can learn to concentrate on one particular idea. Once you have learned how to concentrate, it will become simple for you. The two techniques in this chapter will help you.

The first time my teacher explained these concentration techniques to me, he finished the lesson by telling me to go home and try them. This was a real test for both the techniques and my powers of concentration because I had three children at home and next to our house was a football field. Almost every evening that fall, the school band and cheerleaders practiced. Night games were even noisier. Inevitably, whenever I would chose a time to practice concentrating, the band would start up, cheerleaders would begin yelling, or school was just getting out and students were releasing their pent-up emotions. If I was able to develop my powers of concentration under these conditions, you can learn under any circumstances, too.

The word *concentrate* means the act of drawing to a center. This singleness of purpose is what Jesus referred to when He said, "If therefore thine eye be single, thy whole body shall be full of light." In the Old Testament, Elijah increased the widow's oil and meal through concentration. Like Elijah, when you are concentrating, draw your consciousness to one center so that you are thinking of only one idea. For example, think of the moon. If your thoughts start to wander to your child or business concerns, pull your mind back to the moon as soon as you become aware of this distraction. Concentrate all the time on one idea.

While you are learning the art of concentration, you will draw your mind back again and again to the idea on which you are concentrating. This process of repeatedly drawing your thoughts back will tap and release an energy deep inside of you that has never been touched. When this happens, the energy will spark a current working within the lower part of your mind. This current will surface into the upper part of the mind and all kinds of wonderful things will happen: The emotional blocks that existed in your consciousness for a long time will start to be eliminated. The fear, doubt, and discouragement in your life will start to be dissolved and you will not experience these negative emotions once you have mastered concentration. Through concentration, you become the master of your emotions and the master of your thoughts. You bring into play the incredible powers of your conscious and subconscious minds and the Superior Intelligence.

Develop your powers of concentration for three minutes a day at first, gradually increasing your concentration practice to fifteen minutes a day. Invariably, the first thing most people who want to meditate tell me is that they do not have enough willpower to learn to concentrate. They say, "I just can't sit there that long. I get too itchy; fifteen minutes is just too long." People who express these feelings are certain that they will not be able to learn to concentrate. Naturally, if they *think* that they cannot, they cannot. But if I can, you can. I am a person who thinks quickly. I am always on the go, always eager to do something. I do not like to be idle, yet I have learned the art of concentration. Millions of people have learned to concentrate. You can, too.

After you have learned to meditate with full concentration, you will find that your mind is much keener when you concentrate on ideas and things that need to be done. You will arrive at results more quickly because you will have started to train your mind. Scientists who have researched the mind say that most of us waste our mindpower, using only a fraction of our ability, because our scattered thought patterns do not allow us to look inward for the things we need. This is similar to having to look through a six-foot stack of papers for an answer instead of looking in one file folder in a six-drawer file cabinet. No wonder we have been giving up so easily!

The second concentration technique that you must learn is to stare at a dot for at least five minutes without your eyes watering. Make a dot similar to that shown in Figure 3 by drawing around a penny on an 8½ × 11-inch sheet of paper, then darkening the inside of the dot with a pen or pencil. Place the dot about six feet away from you at eye level and start to stare at it. At first, you will find yourself blinking but it is important that you do *not* blink. You may notice that the dot appears to be jumping up and down. You may even notice that things around the sides of the dot start to disappear. Stare at the dot a few times each day. When your eyes start to water, stop and wait a few hours and then try it again. Do this for two weeks to help you learn to concentrate.

Figure 3. Concentration dot.

WHITE-LIGHT TECHNIQUE

Before you begin learning the simple methods of relaxation, take fifteen minutes or so each day to invoke the white light of the Supreme Intelligence. There is no cost for this wondrous gift, but what valuable rewards you receive when you learn how to use it! Buddha taught that a current full of peace moves through us. He said that once people learn how to invoke it, they would never be hurt again. Confucius said that anyone who used this particular God force would never say an unkind word about, or perform an unkind deed against, his brothers and sisters.

Job spoke of this magnetic energy as the spirit within us. Jesus described the light as the kingdom of God within us. Paul said it was Christ within us, the hope of glory. The mystics of old described this energy force as the white light of God. Some religions describe the white light as the Holy Spirit. Scientists have described this force as an electrical energy that has an intelligence, a vibration of light that fills every cell of our being. No matter what you call the white light, all you have to know is that when you relax, you have the power to contact it.

After you have learned to invoke the white light, you will find that this energy force has powers that are unreal—the white light of the Supreme Intelligence surrounds you and protects your home, your children, and you. Ask for the white light to enter you, heal you, and move through every cell in every part of your body from the top of your head to the tips of your toes.

Begin by standing in the middle of a room; take a few deep breaths to clear your mind, body, and spirit. Then enter the temple of your Higher Self. Attune yourself to this great force in the universe that will renew, inspire, and lift you in your mind and body. Stand with your palms facing upward; ask for this white light to enter you. As this magnetic energy enters your body, your hands will start to feel warm. If at first you do not feel the white light, keep trying. Visualize yourself being surrounded by the warmth and love in the white light and you will eventually experience it.

120

People who ask for the white light of love often receive a healing. You have probably seen or heard about people who have been "zapped" during a healing service in a church. When the white light of the Holy Spirit moves into them, they are zapped, or slain in the spirit, and they faint.

The white light is there and you can invoke it by learning to tune in to the inner stillness within yourself through prayer and meditation. You will feel a spiritual calm down into your soul. Once you receive this inner stillness, you will never again be satisfied without it. And each day as the light and energy of your Higher Self moves into your body, your world will become more peaceful. *You* will become more peaceful.

MEDITATION

After you have mastered the concentration techniques and the white-light technique, the next step is meditation. In most cases, it will take a month or so for you to develop your powers of concentration to this level. A lot depends on how developed your powers of concentration were before you picked up this book. Once you have successfully completed this period of learning how to concentrate and relax yourself, you are ready to meditate.

In meditation, take time to learn how to get in touch with your Higher Self. During meditation, your attention is not directed up or out but *inside* yourself. You are going into your temple to meet your Higher Self—to allow the divine ideas and energy within you to come forth.

Time and Place. Choose a quiet place and a time of day when you will not be disturbed for thirty minutes. Try not to meditate too late in the day, or you may become so relaxed that you fall asleep. You can use any room or part of any room in your house as your special place for meditation. Because this is your special place, you may want to first air out the room. You may wish to decorate the room with fresh flowers, burn incense or a candle, or whatever you want to make this place especially pleasant. If there is a telephone in the room, unplug it or take the receiver off the hook before you begin meditating. If you feel that you might be disturbed, put a sign stating "I'm meditating" on the door to remind people in the house that you should not be disturbed. Also, you must be in the right frame of mind; you cannot be upset, in a bad mood, or feeling hostile when you begin meditation. Remember that you are visiting with your Higher Self.

There are several meditation postures: You may sit on a chair or on the floor, or you may lie down on a bed or on the floor. If you choose to sit in a chair, seat yourself in a comfortable chair that does not restrict the calves of your legs to such an extent that you experience discomfort. When you are comfortable, it is much easier to keep your mind off your body: If you are wearing tight clothing, loosen those ties, belts, bras, or anything else that is restrictive. Also, you may want to cover yourself with a blanket or sheet so that you do not become chilled while you are meditating. Take off your shoes and wiggle your toes. Your feet should be flat on the floor, about six inches apart. Straighten your spine and relax your neck; your head should also be relaxed, not held high. Your hands should be turned palms up, or folded, on your lap. Close your eyes and let your head bend forward a little bit and relax.

You may prefer to sit on the floor in the cross-legged lotus position. If you use this posture, remember to keep your back straight—you may lean against the bottom of a chair or wall—with your head "floating" on top of your spine. Your palms may be up or down on your knees. Close your eyes and bend your head forward slightly. Since this position can be painful if you have not gradually reflexed your legs, you may want to attend yoga classes or read some yoga books before attempting this position.

If you would rather lie down on a bed or the floor, you may certainly do this. Stretch out comfortably, hands crossed over your abdomen, or place them at your sides with palms up. Do not raise your arms over your head or rest your head on your interlaced fingers because this will interfere with the flow of energy through your body. Slowly close your eyes.

Relaxation. Now you are ready for the first step: relaxation. Begin by breathing in while you count to five; hold your breath for another five counts and exhale slowly while you count to five again. Repeat this breathing exercise three times; if you are in a sitting position, do not lean against anything while you are doing the exercise.

Next, you may want to perform self-hypnosis, or auto-suggestion, to release the tension in your shoulders, back, neck, and mind. With your eyes closed, direct all of your attention to your left foot: Feel it becoming heavy; tell it to relax and let go. Do the same with your left calf, and then your left thigh. Once your left leg is feeling very tired, relax your right foot, calf, and thigh. Relax all the tension and let go. Continue by relaxing your back, abdomen, stomach, chest, shoulders, left arm, left hand, right arm, right hand, neck, face, and eye muscles. Your tongue should be in your lower jaw, mouth open slightly, in the same relaxed position as when you sleep. As you are relaxing your body, keep saying to yourself, "Relax. My legs are relaxing and my arms are relaxing; my face is relaxing; my entire body is relaxing." Experience weightlessness; think of yourself as a pat of butter melting in a pan.

While sitting very quietly, begin concentrating on an idea or an ideal, perhaps something that you want in your life such as humility or a positive attitude. At this time, you may also wish to concentrate on a personal affirmation (or one from Chapter 9) that expresses your needs.

Letting Go. The second step in the art of meditation is to let go. Think of the words *let go* and do exactly that: Let go of all of your worries, concerns, and tensions; let go of your anxieties and any negative thoughts that you may have. Let go of the fears or doubts in you. Let go of your problems and feelings of helplessness, self-pity, self-criticism, and self-concern. Let go of all the frustrations, conflicts, and boredom. Breathe in positive thoughts and exhale negative feelings; as you take a few deep breaths, hold each, and release it.

Visualize that there is an opening in the top of your head; through that opening the white light of love is entering your body. While moving through the top of your head, the white light is removing all of the tension and negative thoughts that are holding you back. When the white light reaches your shoulders, it picks up all the stress, burdens, strain, and confusion in life. All of these negative qualities are washed away as the white light of love, peace, and harmony moves straight down through your body. Feel this white light moving through your entire body, moving all the way down to your feet; as it moves, the white light gathers all the negatives in your body.

Floating. The third step in the art of meditation is to experience a feeling of floating. Begin to drift and float; feel free and tranquil and peaceful. While you are floating, think of blue skies and puffy, white clouds; imagine the sea and how beautiful the waves are as they gently lap the shore. Continue floating and begin descending. You may wish to imagine drifting down slowly under a parachute or descending on a series of elevators or escalators. Descend slowly, down, down, down, until you get to the bottom.

Reaching Out. The fourth step in the art of meditation begins when you reach the bottom, the beautiful Valley of Peace where you can reach out to your Higher Self. Imagine your own beautiful, tranquil valley—a place unpolluted by the cares of life. Reach out to your Higher Self in this valley. Use your own words to welcome your Higher Self or say affirmations like these: "I am perfect and this power of the Infinite Intelligence is within me." and "I am. I don't have to understand it, I just know that it is happening. The Infinite Intelligence is flowing through my consciousness and It is in my body. I am unlimited in what I can do with this power. I am feeling joyful and perfect. I am filled with love and happiness." Then fill yourself with tranquility and say, "I am happiness."

After you arrive at this point, let your thoughts drift in and out; eventually, those thoughts will disappear. You will progress into a very peaceful state, a state similar to sleep, but a waking state. At the end of your meditation, slowly walk out of the Valley of Peace and get in touch with your conscious self; open your eyes and stretch. After meditating for thirty minutes, you will feel as rested as if you had been sleeping for six hours. If you meditate for longer than a half hour, you will most likely fall asleep. By using concentration, you can go through all the steps to relax the body, let go, float, and let the Supreme Intelligence come into your being within a half hour.

This is a very simple meditation, a way of attuning yourself to the silence. Once you get into this silence, this peaceful stillness, you will find nothing there. It is a void, and when you come out of it, you will experience a feeling of peace received from deep within yourself.

Meditation is a time of receiving; prayer is a time of asking. When you are in meditation, you are not asking for anything— you are listening to your Higher Self. This is a time to receive energy and truth. If you want to know the truth about a certain situation, concentrate on it and then go ahead and release it, let go, and let the Infinite Intelligence handle it during your meditation. Some people find it helpful to write down their prayer or whatever they want to concentrate on, and then go into their meditation.

The truth is revealed in the silence, not when you are still in your thinking stage. Even though nothing may seem to happen in the silence and you do not hear or receive any great new ideas or guidance, when you learn to practice the silence, you will find that sometimes an idea will be given to you afterward, several hours later. Sometimes you will receive the answer to your problem immediately following the meditation; at other times, the solution will come in a day or two. Because I can never be sure when ideas are going to come to me, I carry a pad and pencil with me and keep a pad and pencil in the car and by the bed so that when I am struck suddenly by a flow of ideas, I am prepared. You may wish to do the same.

One of the unforeseen bonuses of meditation is that many people experience an increasing or an unfolding of their mental-telepathy abilities, clairaudience, and clairvoyance through meditation.

Developing the Art Takes Time. Do not be discouraged if you do not feel that you have succeeded right away. The art of meditation is not acquired in a few weeks; it takes time to develop. It requires practice. Remember that during the period of silence when you are meditating, you try to clear your mind of all thoughts. You have ceased trying to think, to do, to get, or to have; you are just being. This is the true art and where you want to be. While you are learning to meditate, you may wish to use a meditation tape to relax your body and to talk you through a simple meditation. (You may order one of my audiotape cassettes: The address is on page 140.

Even in the early stages, immediately after practicing meditation, you will notice that you not only feel a lot more energetic, enthusiastic, and loving but you will also have a feeling of calm. If you scolded your children earlier in the day, you will find yourself not wanting to raise your voice. You will become easier to get along with and you will want to help people because you are tuning in to the great divine power of your Higher Self. The more you draw from your source, the more you are going to become like the source. You will also find yourself drawn to meditation; you will look forward to your next meditation. It will become a good habit, once a day, every day, for thirty minutes.

The next chapter contains affirmations that can be used for prayer and meditation or to counteract negative vibrations from people around you. These affirmations cover many topics and situations; they will help you attain peace of mind.

NINE

Use Affirmations

An affirmation is a declaration that something is true. When you make this declaration, your subconscious believes it is true. If you repeat an affirmative over and over again, it will manifest as truth in your life. Remember that a thought is something tangible. Thoughts that you send out into the universe eventually reappear in your own life. If you send out positive ideas, you will experience positive reactions. When you think of what you want in your life and persistently affirm this in your conscious mind, this will be fed into your subconscious mind and will eventually come to be.

You may use affirmations not only during prayer and meditation but also to maintain a positive state of mind when doubts and fears panic your mind. Keep repeating the affirmation to yourself until you are calm again. Repeating an affirmation will also protect you when you are part of a group conversation or meeting that degenerates into a negative, backbiting session. By repeating an affirmation at this time, you can keep your subconscious from picking up negativity that would otherwise reappear later in your life.

A HEALING PRAYER

Before you begin using the affirmation technique described in Chapter 1, say the following healing prayer:

> *O Higher Self, You who read all of my thoughts and know me and every detail of my consciousness. Examine me now and know my heart; walk back with me through all the darkened areas of my life and shed light into all of the areas that are still in darkness. I ask to be reborn at this moment, this day. I ask that You heal all the sufferings that I might have experienced during those times of growing up. Erase all of the negatives from my being and allow me to know that I am truly loved by You. Fill me with a sense of Your purpose and of Your love. As I begin my affirmations on this day, I ask that Your blessings be upon them. I thank You because everything I am, I am in You. I am deserving of what I am asking You for. I rest in You and thank You, for I know that it is being done. Amen.*

AFFIRMATIONS

A Basic Affirmation. The following affirmations are offered as examples of the depth, style, and scope of affirmations. Affirmations such as these should be used for every compartment of your life and being.

Use this basic affirmation to sustain your specific daily affirmations:

I now set in motion a new force that will create a steady flow of harmony, health, and happiness in my life and release my potential talents and abilities.

For self-acceptance

- I am a unique, confident, interesting human being receiving an increasing flow of life's abundance. I completely and absolutely accept myself, knowing that any negative conditions in my life are the shadows of thoughts that are now eliminated.
- I hold only good, positive thoughts in my mind about myself, knowing that they will be expressed in my life.

- My perception of my life is heightened, broadened, deepened. Wholeness, beauty, joy, accomplishment, fulfillment, and self-confidence now fill my mind.

- I am perfect; I am whole; I am a child of God.

- I enjoy life, people, and myself and live each moment to the fullest without guilt, self-criticism, or judgment of others.

- What I was yesterday no longer exists. What I am today is what counts.

Whenever you use growth affirmations, be sure to use the words "I am," "I can," or "I will." State that you have an unlimited ability to learn, to develop skills, to stimulate your interests, and to relate to humanity in a productive way.

For spiritual growth

- Every day in every way, I am becoming better and better.

- I act differently because I am different. I am growing each day.

- I am free of any consciousness of personal limitation, lack, doubt, or inferiority.

- I am positive, courageous, and enthusiastic about every moment of my life. I know that holding this thought in my mind will cause my positive experience to expand and the negative experiences to pass quickly into nothingness.

- I accept success as a natural and continuous outgrowth of my reprogrammed attitudes. I enter joyfully into a full expression of this success.

- O Higher Self, purify me; create in me a clean heart; renew in me a right spirit.

In your mind, hold the image of the type of person you want to become. Reinforce this image with specific affirmations.

To develop your personality

- I know that my personality is a reflection of my attitudes. My attitudes are positive; therefore, my personality is positive. People will react to me positively.

- I am _____(fill in the characteristic that you feel is most important for you to acquire: confident, cheerful, enthusiastic, poised, sincere, considerate, attentive, and so on).

- I am completely confident of myself with all people in every situation.

- My life is in divine order. There is a season for all things. My Higher Self knows God's power is working for my good now.

- Let the love of the Infinite Intelligence make me more patient.

For inner peace

- I am a peaceful, relaxed child of God. I am relaxing my body, mind, and spirit. The tension, stress, and strain are no longer there. I relax, release, and let go.

- I face each day with confidence and enthusism, ready to handle any problem with calmness and assurance.

- The peace of my Higher Self is moving through the top of my head, down through my body to the tips of my toes. There is no place within me that does not feel this peace.

- The peace of God moves through all parts of my consciousness. I rest in His peace.

- My emotions are calm. The peaceful indwelling presence of my Higher Self continues to calm me. I am at peace.

- Father, in Thy mercy, in Thy grace, bring to me and my consciousness the awareness of the peace of my Higher Self: That I may say more often, "Father, Thy will be done in and through me day by day."

- The infinite inner peace that abounds in the Supreme Intelligence abounds in me, pouring out this peace through my mind, body, and spirit. I am at peace.

For relationships with others

- I am conscious of only the good in others.

- I am flexible and tolerant in all of my relationships with others.

130

- I love, like, and enjoy _____(name of spouse, family member, or friend).
- I experience joy from my present friendships and pleasure in making new friends.
- I love, believe in, trust, and respect my children so wholeheartedly that I convey this confidence in all my relationships with them.
- I am patient, skillful, and understanding in dealing with all members of my family.
- I love all people and all people love me, without attachment.
- I call on divine love to heal our relationship now. I call on divine love to straighten out and adjust this situation.
- Love changes situations that seem impossible.

To release negative attitudes
and negative aspects of life

- I let go of all limiting thoughts of anxiety and doubt.
- I will not be an emotional cripple, living only half a life because of my negative emotions.
- I am free of all _____(supply the word that fits) malice, hate, jealousy, resentment, grudges, confusion, frustration, tension, conflict, inferiority.
- I surrender every harmful thought, false belief, and negative emotion that has found its way into my body and mind.
- I am free from resentment of all people in all places and all things. In my past and present, I have no room for resentment because my Higher Self fills me through and through.
- I release _____with love and blessings.
- I am filled with love, friendship, understanding, and forgiveness. I hold no resentment, hate, judgment, or self-pity.
- I surrender all my cares and problems to my Higher Self; It knows how to handle these problems correctly and is now working in everyone's best interest. I rest in Its goodness.
- I release my family to you, O Lord. I let go and trust in your decision.

- The negative thoughts and actions of others cannot harm me in any way. I release these thoughts and actions with love to God.

- I forgive you for your actions concerning my loved ones and myself. I release the matter to God, who rights all things.

- You, _____, have no power over me. You are now setting me free. You are releasing me from your life. You are letting go and letting the Supreme Intelligence rule.

- I fully release and forgive you to the forgiving Infinite Intelligence, which has set us free in Its love for us.

- I am forgiven in body, mind, and spirit by the Supreme Intelligence for all my past and present mistakes. I am healed in that belief.

- My Higher Self loves and sees the good in you. You do not wish to hurt me any more. The Higher Self in you sees the love and the good in me. Perfect results now manifest in both of our lives.

- I release you to God. I let go. Let God into your life. Not my will but God's will be done for all in this situation.

- The prejudice I feel is being removed; there is no room in my forgiving heart for bitterness.

- I release all the false ideas and thoughts I have had about myself and others. I am a child of my Higher Self, which has forgiven me all my mistakes. Its thoughts of good about me and others are filling my body at this very moment. I am whole; I am free now and forever.

- I release the situation that is blocking my progress to my Higher Self, which knows all things. My prayer is being answered now.

- All conditions in my life that have brought me pain and resentment are being released by the indwelling Higher Self. I am now at peace in my surroundings.

- My Higher Self now frees me of the people, places, and things that I am attached to from the past and present. My Higher Self will manifest in my life these true desires It has for me.

- There is no room in my life for hatred. I am gentle love. My Higher Self works through me for good always.

- I refuse to have a nervous breakdown. I release you, ⎯⎯⎯⎯⎯⎯, to the Supreme Intelligence fully and freely. I let go and let the Supreme Intelligence have its way in your life.

- I happily and joyously release all old ideas, things, people, and concepts making way for new ideas, things, people, and concepts in my life. This is for the good and is now appearing in my life.

For health

- I am filled with vitality, energy, and physical stamina.

- The perfect life power that flows through every living being is now animating and vitalizing every cell and function of my physical being.

- I think, speak, and act nothing but perfect health.

- May the abundance of my Higher Self fill my mind, soul, and body with the love that brings healing in every manner.

- The divine love of my Higher Self will eradicate any desires that would hinder my body from being physically fit.

- I am perfect, I am whole, I am loved; my body is loved.

- Be Thou merciful, O Supreme Intelligence, in my hour of need for my body, my mind, my soul. Heal Thou my every weakness through my Higher Self that makes me alive in Thee.

- Keep me in the way, O Higher Self, that will bring healing, understanding, and a righteous heart in all my days.

- I do not accept this condition. The Infinite Intelligence's plan for me is perfect health, free of pain. I am healed and I accept this healing now.

- My body is the temple of the living Lord. I am filled with the Infinite Intelligence of God who sees this body only as whole and perfect. I do not accept this diagnosis of incurable disease. I am a perfect child of God and I manifest His perfection now.

- Through the presence of my Higher Self within me, I can do all things. There is no limit to the healing power that is surging through me and healing me now.

- I claim the healing power that expresses itself in me in all ways.

133

Nothing that is not of health and wholeness can get hold of me. I claim that good now in my life.

- I am perfect, I am whole, I am healthy.

To receive blessings

- At this moment in my life, I am an open vessel to the blessings of the Supreme Intelligence; blessings are being received in all phases of my life.

- The earth brings forth its fruits of good harvest.

- I am now receiving all that my Higher Self has that is good for me. There is no limit to Its goodness for me. This goodness is mine; I accept it now.

To overcome obstacles

- My indwelling Higher Self can do all things. I am not limited in any way. My body, mind, and spirit are in divine order.

- I praise divine love that there is a strong, wise way out of this dilemma.

- I can do all things through the power of my subconscious mind.

- This trouble that I am experiencing cannot hurt me; it will help me and make me a finer person. I will have a better character because of it. I am going to look at this problem in the right spirit and I will do what I need to do to get through this experience in the right way. Because of it, I am going to be able to help other people who may come to me with similar problems.

- My body is perfect and whole; every cell is perfect and whole; every bone is perfect and whole.

For weight reduction

- I am reducing and shedding pounds.

Do not use the word *lose* because to lose implies that you will want it back. The subconscious mind will bring back any weight you lose if that word is used.

For improved skills

- I am a _____(golfer, bowler, etc.), able to perform at a high level of excellence.
- I am completely confident, poised, and relaxed.
- I cast out every thought of doubt, fear, or inadequacy about this sport, realizing that these thoughts keep me from participating at the level of my true ability.

For financial help

- My bank account is overflowing. All financial channels are open to me. There is an abundance of good being poured into my life now.
- My Higher Self is powerful and unlimited. It is my true resource, and through It my life will prosper. My demands concerning my situation are now being met.
- God prospers me now.
- By day and by night, I am being prospered in all of my interests.

To sell your house, car, or anything else

- My house (or _____) is sold; it is exactly what the buyer wants and the price is right.

For work situations

- My job is perfect for me and I am perfect for my job.
- The job is mine and I am worthy to have it.

For marriage

- My higher being is drawing to me at this very moment that man (or woman) who will make me happy and whom I will make happy.
- If marriage is for me, then let it be. If you have other plans for me, allow them to manifest in my life. Set me free from this longing within my heart. Set me free to face the future unafraid.

135

To protect everything in your life

- I place you in the hands of the Infinite Intelligence, which desires the highest good for you. And that good will manifest in your own time and in your own way through your Higher Self.

- The Supreme Intelligence works through me, in me, and around me. Nothing in this world can harm me. I am always in Its presence.

- There is nothing in the unseen or seen world that can harm me or make me afraid. My Higher Self is in me and around me. The white light of love protects me from all things.

- I call upon my guardian angel who protects me and watches over me day and night. My way is being cleared for all good things.

For guidance

- My life is being guided by the divine hand of my Higher Self. I can do no wrong in my life. Its ideas work through and in me for the good of all. I release all negative situations in my life that might hinder this guidance.

- Divine love is doing its perfect work in me and through me now.

- O Supreme Intelligence, may the words of my mouth and the meditations of my heart bring into my experience what Thou seest I have need of at this time.

- Divine love is now doing its perfect work in this situation.

- The Infinite Intelligence of my subconscious mind reveals to me my true place in life.

- My subconscious mind knows at all times what particular goals I need to be setting, and my subconscious mind is giving me this information at this very moment.

- I ask my Higher Self to surface at this moment and to show me my true potential in this lifetime.

For faith

- Divine faith moves through all parts of my body and mind. My faith in all things is restored. I am faith; I have faith.

- Surely as I have thought, so shall it come to pass.
- I am a dream of the Supreme Intelligence.
- Whatever you ask in prayer, believe that you have received it and it will be yours.
- Faith is mine. My life is prosperous, my spouse is loving, my children are giving, and I am loving.
- Whatsoever ye shall ask in my name, that will I do.
- In the name of my Higher Self, I ask for _____ to manifest in my life now.
- My Higher Self is producing perfect results for all concerned.
- Supreme Intelligence, use me in whatever way or manner you see fit, that my body may be a living example of Thy love to my brethren.
- May there come into my consciousness more and more the love of the Father, through my Higher Self, day by day.
- May the knowledge of the Lord so fill my life and my body as to make of me a channel in His name.

To invoke the white light
- The white light of my Higher Self shines around and through me. All of my affairs are surrounded by the white light.
- The white light of my Higher Self surrounds my children, home, work, and everything that touches my life in any way, and keeps us safe from any harm.
- The pure white light of my Higher Self protects me in all ways—mentally, physically, and spiritually.
- I project the white light through my body to aid me in restoring health, vitality, and youthful beauty to my entire system.

To attune yourself to the Supreme Intelligence
- The Supreme Intelligence is the only power in the universe, and that power is with me always.
- I am the love of the Infinite Intelligence in expression. I let Its love guide, direct, and inspire me.

- Divine love, expressed through me now, draws to me all that is needed to make me happy and my life complete.
- I give thanks to the divine presence in me that has answered my prayer. In the name of my Higher Self, I give thanks.
- Your will, O Supreme Intelligence, knows best. It is for a greater good in my life. It is working for my intentions now.
- Be still and know that I am God.
- I am perfect and the power of my Higher Self is within me.
- I am. I do not have to understand it; I just know that it is happening. My Higher Self is flowing through my consciousness and in my body. I am unlimited as to what I can do with this power. I am feeling joyful and perfect. I am filled with love and happiness.
- I am happiness.

To be master of your fate
- I am master of my fate—mentally, physically, and spiritually.
- I am the master of my destiny.

A prayer for today
- This is the beginning of a new day. The Infinite Intelligence has given me this day to use as I will. I will use it for good because I am exchanging a day of my life for it! When tomorrow comes, this day will be gone forever, leaving in its place something that I have traded for it. In order that I shall rejoice in the price that I have paid for it, I want that something to be a gain, not a loss; good, not evil; success, not failure.

The Psalms
- Inspired by the Supreme Intelligence, the psalms are an age-old source of comfort and consolation; they have been used for private and public prayer. You will find that the following psalms may be used as affirmations in various situations.

Psalm 4:   If you are in distress
Psalm 5:   Before meditation

Psalm 6:   For health problems
Psalm 7:   If you feel persecuted
Psalm 13:   To ask forgiveness
Psalm 17:   Before sleeping, for perfect harmony in your life
Psalm 23:   When you are lonely
Psalm 25:   For truth and teachings of truth
Psalm 27
and 30:   When you feel afraid, fearful, or troubled
Psalm 31:   For enemies or neighbors who are slandering or lying
Psalm 35:   To plead your case
Psalm 41:   For the poor; for a healing of your soul
Psalm 67:   For all nations
Psalm 86:   For the poor and needy
Psalm 88:   For the dying
Psalm 91:   For God as your soldier
Psalm 103:   To bless God's holy name and all who work for Him
Psalm 116:   To give thanks for an answered prayer
Psalm 146:   For comfort in adversity

If you would like to receive information about my video-tapes and audiotape cassettes on pyramid power, healing, goal setting, listening, communications, the higher consciousness, prayer and affirmations, and the subconscious mind, please write to:

Patricia Mischell
P.O. Box 1238
Cincinnati, Ohio 45201

Recommended Reading List

Bloodworth, Venice, *Key to Yourself.* Marina Del Ray, CA: DeVorss & Company, 1970.

Bristol, Claude, *Magic of Believing.* Englewood Cliffs, NJ: Prentice-Hall, Inc., 1982.

————, *T.N.T., The Power Within You.* Englewood Cliffs, NJ: Prentice-Hall, Inc., 1954.

Cousins, Norman, *Anatomy of an Illness, as Perceived by the Patient.* New York: W.W. Norton & Company, 1979.

Fromm, Eric, *The Art of Loving.* New York: Harper & Row Publishers, Inc., 1974.

Hill, Napolean, *Think and Grow Rich.* New York: Fawcett Book Group, 1979.

Kübler-Ross, Elisabeth, *On Death and Dying.* New York: Macmillan Publishing Company, 1969.

Maltz, Maxwell, *Psycho-Cybernetics.* Englewood Cliffs, NJ: Prentice-Hall, Inc., 1960.

Mandino, Og, *The Greatest Miracle in the World*. New York: Bantam Books, Inc., 1977.

Mandino, Og, *The Greatest Salesman in the World*. New York: Bantam Books, Inc., 1974.

Murphy, Joseph, *Miracle of Mind Dynamics*. Englewood Cliffs, NJ: Prentice-Hall, Inc., 1964.

————, *The Power of Your Subconscious Mind*. Englewood Cliffs, NJ: Prentice-Hall, Inc., 1963.

————, *These Truths Can Change Your Life*. Marina Del Ray, CA: DeVorss & Company, 1982.

Peale, Norman Vincent, *The Power of Positive Thinking*. New York: Fawcett Book Group, 1978.

Ponder, Catherine, *Pray and Grow Rich*. Englewood Cliffs, NJ: Prentice-Hall, Inc., 1968.

Schuller, Robert, *Living Positively One Day at a Time*. Old Tappan, NJ: Fleming H. Revell Company, 1981.